PERFECT PLANT,
PERFECT GARDEN

ANNE SCOTT-JAMES

PERFECT PLANT, PERFECT GARDEN

conran
OCTOPUS

Perfect Plant

First published as *The Best Plants for
Your Garden* by Conran Octopus Limited
A part of Octopus Publishing Group
2–4 Heron Quays
London E14 4JP
www.conran-octopus.co.uk

Reprinted 1995, 2001

Managing Editor Mary Davies

Assistant Editor Katherine Dunn

Picture research Nadine Bazar

Art Director Mary Evans

Art Editor Cherriwyn Magill

Design Assistant James Alexander

Illustrator Valerie Price

Production Michel Blake

ISBN 1 85029 799 1

Typeset by Bookworm Typesetting

Printed and bound in Hong Kong

CONTENTS

INTRODUCTION

In my view, no garden plant has absolute virtue. A plant may be beautiful in form, charming in colour, and vigorous by nature, but it is only a good plant if it is in harmony with your garden. If it fits well with your soil and climate, if it is happy with the light or shade, dryness or moisture, you can offer it, and if it blends easily with the plants around it, only then is it worthy of your love and care. That is why, in choosing plants for this book, I have not divided them, like a catalogue, into sections for shrubs, perennials, climbers, bulbs and so on, but have placed each plant according to its needs. Have you a dry, sunny garden? Or a garden with a squelchy pond? Or a peaty woodland? Or a garden in the shade of buildings? Or a garden robbed by hungry trees? Then I hope you will find here some plants to please you which should flourish in your particular site.

In choosing, I have turned first to the plants I know best, those which are widely grown in Britain, but of course gardening today is international. Plants have been crossing the continents for centuries, and the gardens of Britain are enriched with species and varieties from the United States, China, Japan, South Africa, Australia, and every other country with a temperate climate. English primroses grow readily under Chinese viburnums, the trilliums of North America under English oaks. I have seen the same happy mixing of plants in gardens in many parts of the world.

In choosing plants for what is largely a personal book, one is naturally influenced by one's own tastes, and I had better come clean and admit to some predilections. In general, I incline to plant species rather than cultivars, though not to a foolish extent. I love the simplicity, the *rightness*, of species, especially in a wild garden, but I appreciate that many shrubs have marvellous cultivars, and that the mixed border would look skimpy if all the plants were from the wild – there is no wild delphinium, as far as I know, worthy to stand up with lilies and shrub roses. And in the terrace or balcony garden, it is usually cultivars which give what is most needed in a restricted space – a long period of display.

Then, I am always a pushover for scented plants, even if they are small and inconspicuous, like some of the tiny irises. And I love plants which have personal associations; perhaps I have seen them in friendly places, or read about them in favourite books, or seen them in beautiful pictures. I like *Anemone blanda* because I have seen it growing wild in Italy, and the crown imperial because the eloquent seventeenth-century gardener, John Parkinson, admired it above all other flowers, and the cabbage roses of French flower paintings. Every gardener of long experience will be partly guided by sentiment. (The young gardener with no memory bank must experiment, and perhaps change his mind as time goes by.) Good garden writing has always been a particularly strong influence on me, and I have quoted a few outstanding authors throughout the book – John Parkinson, William Robinson, Gertrude Jekyll, Reginald Farrer, W.J. Bean, Vita Sackville-West, Margery Fish and, in our own time, Graham Stuart Thomas and Christopher Lloyd.

So much for my idiosyncrasies. In the main, I hope I have been objective, and I have tried to choose plants with certain solid qualities. For example, a worthwhile plant must have good garden value, giving pleasure over much of the year. A spring-flowering shrub with autumn fruits or colour takes precedence over a shrub with neither. A repeat-flowering rose counts above a once-only rose, however beautiful. Plants with fine foliage, like hostas, geraniums and alchemilla, will enhance a garden even when out of flower, as will some of the rose species, which compensate for their brief flowering season with sprays of fern-like leaves throughout the summer.

Some plants have won a place in the book because they flower when they are particularly welcome. Nerines look fresh and springlike when most flowers are tired and autumnal. Winter-flowering plants inspire special gratitude, and many last a long time, like the Chinese shrub *Viburnum farreri* and the winter hellebores, which are undismayed by frost or snow. This brings me to the vexed question of hardiness. How hardy do you want your plants to be? I think some gardeners are so reluctant to take a risk that they miss many beautiful things. Of course, one wants trees and slow-growing plants to stand up indefinitely to the local climate and last for ever, but if a fast-growing plant gives years of pleasure and then succumbs to a fiendish winter I do not think one should shed too many tears. In recent bad winters my cistuses have taken terrible knocks, but they are easily replaced, and I shall chance them again. And plants seemingly dead often revive after a period. Almost every year we hear wails from the Mediterranean that all the vines, or lemons, or mimosa trees are dead, but there still seem to be plenty about. Either they have not died, or it has been possible to replace the stock.

Another virtue which many gardeners look for in a plant is good value for cutting, and I have mentioned this from time to time. Everyone likes fresh flowers in the house and though I am not myself a dedicated 'flower arranger', I can fill at least one little jug in every week of the year, and many more in spring and summer.

Plant association is an art which I personally find very difficult, for the most thoughtful planting can go wrong if one member of the group fails. But, with trepidation, I have suggested associations for many plants in the book, often because I have enjoyed them in other gardens, not my own. I think that visiting gardens is one of the best ways of learning, and I never visit one without taking a notebook and jotting down the names of plants which have been beautifully grouped with an eye for height, habit and leaf shape as well as colour. Though I like to record colour schemes, this is a subject on which I would never be dogmatic, for it is a matter of personal taste. Some gardeners aim for brilliance, with colours contrasting rather than harmonizing, and there is a case for this, especially in a town garden, where the surroundings may be drab; and in high summer the eye can accept stronger colour than in spring. Strong colour was the strength of the Victorian garden, when a wealth of new hybrids brought opportunities for a blaze unknown before. Today, we are more sensitive to the beauty of a quiet garden, with many foliage plants, many white flowers, many grey and silver leaves to soften the bright colours of summer. I do not say that one school

is better than another – a good garden is the one you like – but it is worth considering all the possibilities before choosing your plants. The only colour scheme I personally dislike is pink with yellow – how often is a sheet of daffodils spoiled by a canopy of pink flowering cherries overhead. My own worst disaster was when, by an oversight, a group of yellow loosestrife ran wild among pink roses.

Most of the plants I have chosen are obliging plants. I won't pretend that they are totally labour-saving, for this quality is rare, and if you do not enjoy working the soil and weeding and pruning, you might as well call in a contract gardener. But where there are two similar plants, one of which needs staking while the other does not (as with achilleas), I have chosen the variety with the stronger stems. And I have not included those delectable but rampant spring clematis which climb to the eaves, because they are difficult to train and need strong nerves on a ladder. Some of the plants in the book are so adaptable that they will grow in a variety of conditions, and I have puzzled as to where to place them. For instance, I have allotted alchemilla to the section on plants for moist shade, but it will grow almost anywhere, and many plants in the sunny sections will flower well in light shade – I have mentioned this in nearly every case. On the other hand, I have included a tiny handful of plants, like *Meconopsis betonicifolia*, which are frankly difficult to grow, but will cause ecstasy if you can pull them off. Regard them as an aberration on my part.

The techniques of gardening are not the main subject of this book, but I would like to record a few reflections.

When buying plants, it is important to buy only the best, and not to be stingy about expenditure. A weakly plant, or a bad form of a plant, or just a dull plant, is never worth its space. It was Harold Nicolson who wrote to his wife, Vita Sackville-West, creator of the paradise garden at Sissinghurst Castle, 'I think the secret of your gardening is simply that you have the courage to abolish ugly or unsuccessful flowers.'

Having bought good plants, care for them well, especially in their first season, when they may need regular watering until the roots are established. And, if possible, mulch your garden once or even twice a year, covering the soil between the plants with manure, compost, leafmould, peat or crushed bark, or any decayed vegetable matter available to you. All of these will preserve valuable moisture if applied when the soil is wet, and some will also provide good food.

When I started gardening a long time ago, a great woman gardener said to me, 'Get to know your garden. Understand its climate, soil and nature as you would the character of a child', and she was right. Every garden, whether a rolling landscape or a suburban rectangle, has a *genius loci*, and the gardener who understands his site is on the road to success.

Anne Scott-James.

7

THE SUNNY GARDEN

Every region of the temperate world has contributed to the wide range of plants –
shrubs, roses, herbaceous perennials, bulbs, annuals and biennials – that thrive
in the sunny garden.

In choosing plants for the sunny parts of your garden, it is sensible to consider in what area of the world each plant grows wild, or, if you are growing a garden variety (or cultivar), to find out where the species comes from. I believe strongly in giving each plant a habitat as near as possible to its natural home. Sun-loving plants grow in many different terrains – open meadows, peaty bogs, limestone mountains, sandy heaths, gritty screes, even deserts – but they share one characteristic, that they will not flower well without plenty of light. In areas where the heat is torrid, sun-loving plants develop their own systems of management, such as storing water in succulent leaves, but we are dealing here with plants from temperate climates, which may not get as much sun in Britain as they

ABOVE Most plants with grey foliage are sun-lovers and thrive in light, well-drained soils. Pink and red flowers are particularly effective when shown against the soft colour of their leaves.

RIGHT High summer is when the perennials of a herbaceous border are at their peak. Here the blue delphiniums mix with yellow ligularias and hemerocallis.

ABOVE The wide range of plants suitable for the sunny garden allows scope for many colour schemes. A combination of white, pink and blue is an attractive alternative to the yellow composites of summer.

enjoy at home, but can adapt if we put them in appropriate quarters.

Of these, roses, native to the whole northern hemisphere, including the Arctic, are amazingly versatile, and will grow almost anywhere given sun and good treatment. The *maquis* of the Mediterranean provides us with a wonderful range of aromatic, evergreen shrubs and subshrubs, such as lavenders, rosemaries, myrtles, cistuses, sages, which will prosper with us if given their natural conditions of good drainage and preferably some lime. North America, with its wonderful flora, is particularly rich in composite daisy-plants which cross the Atlantic well. South Africa sends us sensational bulbs, like agapanthus, from

which our nurserymen have bred varieties hardier than the species. From the acid bogs of the Himalayas come primulas for growing beside sunny streams and pools. From China we have hundreds of flowering shrubs, and from the Alps and other mountains of the world come certain alpines which will take to life in raised, gritty beds in the English garden. Eucalyptus and hebes from Australia and New Zealand make themselves at home here if we give them some shelter. The sun-lovers of South America are mostly too tender for the outdoor garden in Britain, but even these we grow in quantity as bedding plants.

Having chosen the sun-loving plants which will suit your garden best, and

Sunny herbaceous borders flanking a narrow stone path are planted in a rich colour scheme of blues, yellows and many shades of green but occasional white flowers add highlights.

RIGHT A pattern of low clipped box adds a formal note to a luxuriant planting scheme dominated by pink, blue and white.

peonies) will flower in light shade, though not so freely as in sun. Some plants from countries with acid soil (like Japanese hostas) will acccept lime without complaint. Lime-lovers (like cistus) will grow in acid soil if it is not too heavy. Some of the easier alpines, accustomed to the gritty soil of a scree, will fit into ordinary soil in a mixed border. Many plants from hot countries, like Greece, prove perfectly hardy because they go underground in winter. Even an abutilon from Brazil may flourish on a sunny wall. In the long run, your greatest asset is your own feeling for plants and your own experience, which often belies the accepted wisdom.

The plants in the following chapter are all chosen as reasonably easy denizens of the sunny garden, in normal, dry, or wet conditions.

A giant among biennials, *Heracleum mantegazzianum*, although short-lived, makes a plant of noble proportions to combine with sun-loving perennials and shrubs in a wild garden where the soil is moist.

decided on the most suitable site, well-drained or boggy, acid or alkaline, you must think about their cultivation. The important thing is to start them off well, planting shrubs and perennials with grit/manure/sand/peat/leafmould/bonemeal, according to their needs, and to cosset them for the first two years, especially in the matter of water, for they may dry out before they are well established. Plants which need constant watering after that are not practicable, in my view, unless the gardener has nothing better to do than walk around with a hose. The best way to keep perennial plants supplied with moisture is to mulch them, applying blankets of decayed compost, peat or pulverized bark when the soil is wet to keep the moisture *in* when sun and wind are doing their best to take the moisture *out*. Water only if plants are clearly flagging. Annuals, of course, having shallow roots, must be watered with particular care.

Having said this – that plants should be well sited and well looked after when young – it is uplifting to find how many plants manage perfectly well in conditions which are not ideal. Many sun-lovers (like

In a sunny dry corner of a large garden, shrubs and perennials that give a long season of interest are grown closely together; the grouping looks natural and weeding is reduced to a minimum.

Acer palmatum 'Osakazuki' is a slow-growing deciduous shrub or small tree that is rarely more than 6 feet (1.8 m) high. The elegant leaves turn brilliant orange and scarlet in autumn.

Acer palmatum 'Osakazuki'

Much of the pleasure of plants grown for autumn colour lies in watching the gradual suffusion of the leaves, so if you are choosing a Japanese maple I suggest one which is green in summer rather than the ever-purple varieties which can be monotonous to the eye. There are many acers with fresh green leaves in summer, deeply dissected and exquisite in shape, which turn slowly to an autumn blaze of orange and scarlet, and 'Osakazuki' is one of the most spectacular. A slow-growing, rounded, deciduous shrub or small tree, not usually taller than 6 feet (1.8 m), it can be massed in a large garden, as at the Westonbirt Arboretum in Gloucestershire, or Sheffield Park in Sussex, or grown as a single specimen in a small garden, perhaps in a lawn near the house. Another widely grown, taller Japanese

Acer palmatum

maple, of more delicate colouring, is 'Senkaki', the coral-bark maple, with pink stems and light green leaves which turn pinkish gold in autumn. It needs a dark background, perhaps a conifer, to set off the pastel pink, green and gold.

These maples need a rich, moist, preferably peaty soil, and protection from cold winds. They do well in town gardens provided they are not planted against an east wall, where morning sun on night frost could scorch the leaves. Though they are often listed as lime-tolerant, I would not myself chance these maples in alkaline soil.

Actinidia kolomikta

It looks as though the gardeners in *Alice in Wonderland* who painted the roses had passed by and splashed the green leaves of this sensational climber with pink and white paint. They have an artistic and erratic variegation of three colours which

I have seen in no other plant.

It is a deciduous shrub growing up to 12 feet (3.6 m) or more, with all the interest in the foliage. The large leaves, up to 6 inches (15 cm) long, are heart-shaped and pointed, and unfold in late spring with some of the tips stark white and some peppermint pink, the colours painted in straight blocks, not melting

Actinidia kolomikta is a deciduous climber that will reach a height of 12 feet (3.6 m) or more. In full sun, the large leaves variegate spectacularly, the green splashed with creamy white and pink.

Actinidia kolomikta

softly into one-another. The leaves do not variegate until the plant is several years old. There are inconspicuous but faintly scented white flowers in early summer.

If it is to variegate, the plant must have full sun and does best on a south or west wall, and needs some support. Though tolerant of a little lime, it will grow more quickly in a neutral loam. It is a bushy plant, with branches to the ground, and does not call for underplanting, though pink and white double Chinese peonies would look wonderful nearby.

Anemone blanda

This cheerful blue anemone, or wind-flower, times its arrival neatly for the moment when the snowdrops fade, just when you are looking for another wave of spring bulbs, and continues to flower over several weeks. It looks best natural-ized under small trees, like whitebeams, or among deciduous shrubs, though in the well-drained alkaline soil which it prefers it will also seed itself in grass. (Vita Sackville-West found a spontaneous col-ony in her orchard at Sissinghurst.) It will grow in sun or light shade and seeds freely, but can be a nuisance if it takes to your flower-beds, from which it is best removed. The species is mid-blue, a starry flower with many petals and typical feathery anemone leaves, but there are pink and mauve forms, and an attractive white one with larger flowers.

If you have not the space to let *A. blanda* naturalize, plant the rhizomes 4 inches (10 cm) apart in a special bed

Anemone blanda is easy to naturalize and the starry flowers, about 6 inches (15 cm) high, combine well with those of other dwarf bulbs. The usual colour is blue but there are pink, magenta and white forms.

packed with other small spring bulbs — muscari, irises, tulip species, and perhaps some polyanthus. By summer, this bed will look a bit of a mess, but planting for a special season creates a unique picture which successional planting cannot achieve, and massed spring bulbs recall the enchantment of Botticelli's *Primavera*.

Anemone blanda

Anemone × *hybrida*

This clumsily named herbaceous plant is what we all know as 'Japanese anemones', but is a hybrid of several wild species, and we have to accept this nomenclature.

It is a beautiful plant, flowering from late summer into autumn, and has many

ing yellow stamens, and have the candid, innocent look usually found only in spring flowers. They grow in profusion on branching stems about 3 feet (90 cm) tall. The leaves, which begin to make their mark long before flowering time, are like vine-leaves. These anemones are said to do best in heavy soil, but are rampant on my

Anemone × *hybrida*

both of them single-flowered, for in the double forms the anemone's essential simplicity is always lost.

The hybrid Japanese anemones, *Anemone* × *hybrida*, are valuable hardy perennials that flower in late summer and autumn. 'Honorine Jobert', which grows to about 3 feet (90 cm), is a fine single white.

virtues and one vice. Taking the virtues first, it is hardy, healthy and perennial, delightful in flower and leaf, and requires no staking. The vice – it is dreadfully invasive, and in a mixed border will turn up in the middle of your favourite rosebush, or at the front of the border with your dwarf campanulas. It is therefore safest to grow it among shrubs.

The flowers are shallow saucers with soft pink or pure white petals surround-

light soil, so I think they will grow anywhere, but are better in sun than shade. They are slow starters, so do not expect great rewards for at least two years. Eventually, the roots go very deep, and they resent being moved, so give much thought to their placing. Plant them 2 feet (60 cm) apart.

Of a number of varieties on the market, I commend 'Queen Charlotte', a rosy pink, and the white 'Honorine Jobert',

Aster × *frikartii* '**Mönch**'

There are many handsome Michaelmas daisies for the autumn border, but this is by far the best, a hardy perennial with a number of exceptional qualities. It is less stiff and bushy than most Michaelmas daisies; the branching stems, carrying large, lavender-blue, starry flowers with yellow centres, are slightly floppy, though not lax enough to need staking. It does not require frequent division, for it increases slowly, and is unlikely to outgrow its space for three or four years. And it does not suffer from mildew.

Plant the daisies 16 inches (40 cm) apart in good, enriched soil in a sunny place, preferably in spring. (I am coming increasingly to favour spring planting for perennials, after a number of devastating winters.) Give an annual mulch in autumn, working a compost or rotted manure between the plants.

The soft blue of *Aster* x *frikartii* 'Mönch' makes a pastel picture with pink Japanese anemones (*Anemone* x *hybrida*), or it can be used, more strikingly, with plants of tawny colouring, such as *Sedum* 'Autumn Joy', which is pink in the bud but turns to rich bronze, or with orange *Crocosmia*. At Sissinghurst, the long Moat Walk, leading to the moat from the Cottage Garden, is

Among the Michaelmas daisies, *Aster × frikartii* is outstanding. It grows to a height of about 30 inches (75 cm), does not need staking, flowers profusely in autumn and does not suffer from mildew.

The fragrant flowers of *Buddleja alternifolia* appear in mid-summer, clustered along the arching branches. This deciduous shrub, which can grow to 12 feet (3.6m) has a graceful weeping habit.

bordered down one side with a narrow bed of 'Mönch', with flaming *Parrotia persica* trees behind to make a glorious autumn splash.

Graham Thomas names this Michaelmas daisy as one of the six best plants 'which should be in every garden', high praise from a master of perennial planting.

Buddleja alternifolia

This deciduous Chinese shrub (formerly spelt *Buddleia*) has the graceful habit of a weeping willow. A vigorous grower, it will reach 12 feet (3.6 m) or more in height in a few years, and in mid-summer the slender, arching branches will be entirely covered with clusters of small, mauve, scented flowers. When not in flower, the shrub is a waterfall of dove-grey, for the narrow, alternate, pale-green leaves are glaucous on the under-side, while in the rarer form, 'Argentea',

the effect is silver. Reginald Farrer, famous authority on alpine plants, discovered the shrub in north-west China in 1915, and compared it to 'a gracious

Buddleja alternifolia

small-leaved weeping willow'.

This buddleja needs a sunny position and will thrive in any good garden soil. The ideal place for it is on top of a bank, with the branches cascading down. It can also be trained as a small tree. It must not be pruned in spring, like the autumn-flowering *B. davidii*, for it flowers on the wood developed the previous summer.

A shrub of such elegant habit and colouring looks best with harmonious, rather than contrasting, plants. The giant sea-kale, *Crambe cordifolia*, with its forest of tiny white flowers rising on tall stalks from large dark green leaves, looks well in front of it, and the equally tall meadow-rue, *Thalictrum speciosissimum*, with heads of fluffy yellow flowers, would complete a picture of pastel delicacy.

Campanula lactiflora is a hardy herbaceous perennial for the mid-summer border, where it combines well with roses and lilies. The stems, which are 4 feet (1.2 m) high, carry large heads of blue flowers.

Campanula lactiflora

This tall elegant campanula is a worthy companion for roses, lilies, delphiniums and other sumptuous plants of the mid-summer border. A hardy herbaceous perennial, it carries large branching heads of starlike blue flowers on stalks 4 feet (1.2 m) high, which are thick with toothed, pointed leaves. The best of several good blue forms is the lavender-blue 'Prichard's Variety', and there is a charming soft pink called 'Loddon Anna'.

This capanula needs space and looks best in a large group of at least five plants with pink, apricot, white, or other blue flowers round about. At all costs avoid yellow, a killer to pastel colours, especially the delicate pink of 'Loddon Anna'. Tall shrub roses, like the purple-pink, double bourbon 'Madame Isaac Pereire' or the hybrid musk 'Cornelia', with clusters of

Campanula lactiflora

coral-pink double flowers, would make a billowy background for the campanulas. White lilies could be planted beside them, and a silver foliage plant, like *Stachys olympica*, at their feet. This would be a cool, refreshing colour scheme in the long hot days when the rampant yellow

composite plants are trying to capture the garden. Plant the campanulas 2 feet (60 cm) apart in rich, well-drained soil in a sunny bed, and leave them in peace for several years.

Chaenomeles speciosa

This splendid deciduous shrub, once known to the amateur as 'japonica', is a Japanese flowering quince. It can be grown on a wall, preferably (though not necessarily) facing south, where it may climb to 8 feet (2.4 m) and spread to double that distance. It looks neat and

formal trained round the lower windows of a house, a change from the sprawly climbing roses and honeysuckles. Any good soil will suit it.

The scarlet flowers, cupped like apple blossom, bloom in clusters from very early to late spring. In early summer, when all the flowers are over, the tricky

The Japanese flowering quince, Chaenomeles speciosa, is a deciduous shrub that will grow to 8 feet (2.4 m) or more against a wall. There are red, pink and white forms as well as the usual scarlet.

business of pruning should be done. When the plant is young, just cut off any branchlets which are growing outward from the wall; once a network of branches is established, cut out unwanted wood, and also spur back the previous season's shoots to two or three buds.

There are varieties of *C. speciosa* in a number of shades of red and pink, some with double flowers, but, next to the scarlet species, my favourite is the pure white 'Nivalis'. Cottage peonies, with their strong green foliage and double red flowers, are effective planted at the shrub's feet.

I believe the fruit can be made into quince jelly, but I admit that I have not tried it as I always have enough crab apples for this worthy activity.

The Shasta daisy, Chrysanthemum maximum, is a hardy herbaceous perennial that gives a long display of marguerite-like flowers on stems 3 feet (90 cm) high in mid-summer. There are single and double forms.

nearer to the wild marguerites of our locality which kindly seed in my banks of rough grass, but if you like the doubles there is a handsome variety called 'Wirral Supreme'. Both single and double forms last well if cut for the house, and need nothing more than green foliage to make a cool, summery bouquet.

Plant the daisies in clumps of three placed 2 feet (60 cm) apart. They increase rapidly and should be divided every other spring. Being shallow-rooted, they may need watering in dry weather.

Chaenomeles speciosa

Chrysanthemum maximum

It is impossible to have too many white daisies in the garden, and *Chrysanthemum maximum*, the Shasta daisy, is one of the most charming, a vigorous herbaceous perennial like a large marguerite. The single white flowers with yellow centres on stems 3 feet (90 cm) high succeed each other over many weeks in mid-summer. It is also satisfying to have plenty of white in the summer border to offset the blues of delphiniums and campanulas and the bright magenta of *Geranium psilostemon*. It is often known as *C.* × *superbum*; my own variety is called 'Everest'.

I confess to preferring the single to the double Shasta daisies, because they are

Chrysanthemum maximum

Clematis tangutica

This Asiatic species is a born scrambler, more at home among the branches of a shrub than on a trellis. Hardy and deciduous, it can climb to 20 feet (6 m), producing a succession of small, nodding yellow flowers, consisting of four thick-textured sepals, for two to three months in autumn. As each flower fades, it turns into a silky seedhead, flowers and seedheads together smothering the host plant in a confetti of yellow and silver. The leaves are light green, deeply cut, and very graceful.

A problem is choosing the host shrub, for the clematis can strangle any but the sturdiest bush. I find that the winter-flowering *Viburnum farreri* can take the strain, its pink scented flowers taking over when the clematis has finally rung down the curtain. It gives the clematis the shade at the roots which it requires, but allows it to scramble upwards to flower in the sun. Reginald Farrer, referring to the wild, untidy growth of *C. tangutica*, likened the whole clematis family unkindly to the wild-haired character Struwwelpeter of the German children's book, forgetting the full import of this sadistic tale.

Like many clematis, *C. tangutica* likes well-drained alkaline soil, and it should be pruned in early spring. It is impossible to prune such a muddled grower shoot by shoot; just take a handful of shoots at a time and cut them to a suitable place above the old wood, cutting above a pair of buds where you can.

Clematis tangutica

Cotinus coggygria 'Royal Purple'

I am not usually an admirer of purple-leaved trees and shrubs, which look alien in a green country, but the Venetian sumach or smoke tree in the variety 'Royal Purple' makes such a good background to border flowers, especially white ones, that it is an exception.

A large, rounded, deciduous shrub

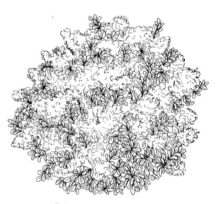

Cotinus coggygria

An autumn-flowering species, *Clematis tangutica* can reach a height of 20 feet (6m). The nodding flowers, which consist of thick lemon-yellow sepals, are followed by silky seedheads.

growing to 8 feet (2.4 m) or more, it is a bushy mass of dark purple leaves all through the summer, changing to light red in autumn. The leaves are an unusual shape, being almost circular. In mid-summer, large feathery plumes of tiny purple flowers burst from the bush like puffs of smoke, and turn grey before they fade. The 'Royal Purple' variety enhances the whiteness of roses, lilies, delphiniums, mallows and other tall border plants, though pale pinks and blues also look well

The foliage of 'Royal Purple', a dark form of the smoke tree, *Cotinus coggygria*, contrasts with the immature leaves of *Eucalyptus gunnii*. The deciduous smoke tree grows to about 8 feet (2.4m).

against the sombre background. There could be silver plants, like *Santolina incana*, in the foreground.

The species, *C. coggygria*, has green leaves and stronger autumn colour, and is recommended by the famous gardening author, Christopher Lloyd, as a specimen for a lawn. The flowers turn pink in late summer, and he says that the sparkle of dew on the pink blossom in early morning is a great gardening experience.

Plant *Cotinus* in poorish soil, and if you site it at the back of a mixed border, keep manure well away from your shrub.

Crocus tommasinianus

One day Mr E. A. Bowles, plantsman extraordinary and crocus expert of the century, woke up with a raging toothache, went out into the garden, and saw a sea of *Crocus tommasinianus* in full bloom. Such was his delight that the toothache vanished.

This charming crocus species, a native of Dalmatia, has lavender-blue flowers with bright gold stamens, the inner petals

a little darker than the outer ones. It flowers in early spring, before the larger Dutch hybrids, and is the perfect crocus for naturalizing. It clumps up quickly and seeds everywhere, in turf, in beds, even in paving. In the first year, when just one or two flowers emerge from every bulb, wind and rain can knock them about, but do not be dismayed. Somehow, when clumps are formed with many flowers to each, they seem to hold each other up. There is a dark violet variety called 'Whitewell Purple' and a few drifts grown among the paler crocuses will make a rich pattern in a sunny stretch of turf. Plant the bulbs 3 inches (7.5 cm) deep, not too near together, leaving room for the clumps to develop.

One of the best dwarf spring-flowering bulbs for naturalizing is *Crocus tommasinianus*, with lavender-blue flowers about 3 inches (7.5cm) high. Clumps stand up well to rough weather.

Daphne mezereum is a reasonably hardy deciduous shrub that grows to about 5 feet (1.5m). In early spring the bare branches carry dense clusters of pale or deep pink fragrant flowers. There is also a white form. This daphne does well on limy soils.

Daphne mezereum

This is one of the easier daphnes to grow in a sunny or lightly shaded garden, being hardy except in the bitterest winters; it likes a good, well-drained soil, preferably with some lime. It is a small, erect deciduous shrub flowering in early spring, dense clusters of typical purplish-pink daphne flowers crowding on the previous year's shoots. The leaves come

Daphne mezereum

later, and there are scarlet berries in mid-summer. Like other daphnes, it has a strong, sweet scent. It is a native of Europe and Asia Minor, and some say of Britain, but this is doubtful.

The nymph Daphne was something of a heroine in ancient Greece, being one of Apollo's rare amatory failures. He pursued her and was rejected, the nymph calling on the gods for rescue. They turned her into a daphne bush, though of which species I have not been able to discover.

The most beautiful planting of *Daphne mezereum* I have seen is in a Cotswold garden, where it is grown as a low hedge, but I have also admired it as a specimen bush by a cottage front door, underplanted with snowdrops – it has been considered a cottage plant for hundreds of years.

There is an equally charming white form, 'Alba', with yellow berries.

Delphinium hybrids

Of all the plants in this book the garden delphinium has travelled furthest from the various species in the wild. More than a century of intensive breeding has produced the tall, large-flowered hybrids which are so popular today, and which make one of the most theatrical exhibits every year at the Chelsea Flower Show, usually rewarded with a Gold Medal.

The large hybrids are flamboyant plants of varying height, commonly 5 feet (1.5 m) tall or more, growing in huge spikes crowded with flat rosettes of flower, single or double, often with a contrasting eye. The most familiar colour is sky-blue, but today there is a wide range of blue, purple, pink, white, yellow, and – the breeder's dream realized – red. This last is not yet on the general market, but will be within a few years. The leaves of delphiniums are deeply cut and make attractive mounds of light green.

The hybrid delphiniums are classic tall herbaceous perennials for the border, growing to a height of about 5 feet (1.5 m). They are valued for their range of blues but colours include white, yellows and red.

Delphinium hybrid

The unsolved problem with delphiniums is staking. Even the shorter varieties need canes, for twigs are not strong enough. Christopher Lloyd stakes each plant with two canes in the famous Long Border at his home, Great Dixter, in Sussex, but not until the stalks are 3 feet (90 cm) tall, and then not to the full height of the flower. He says that any flower which is so bloated that it needs a cane to the top should be thrown out. Other gardeners stake all the way, with a cane to every spike, so that the delphinium border is a parade of flowers and canes, nature being quite forgot.

There is another range of garden varieties to please those who do not hold that big is beautiful, the Belladonna hybrids, which are shorter, more branched, and smaller in flower than the jumbos.

Delphiniums are a staple element in the herbaceous border during its midsummer zenith, along with Shasta daisies, *Thalictrum*, lilies, lupins, campanulas and many more. Miss Jekyll, in her celebrated long border at Munstead Wood, mixed the highly-bred giants with cottage plants, and lavender, catmint, pinks, grasses and even wild soapwort rubbed shoulders with delphiniums, lilies, cannas and dwarf rhododendrons.

Delphiniums like full sun and rich soil with no lime, or just a little, and if cut down after flowering there will be fresh leaves and probably side-shoots of flowers. Plant in groups 2 feet (60 cm) apart. I have not suggested varieties, though

the range is always large and exciting, because the same ones are not available every year. A sound way to choose is from a catalogue, or, better still, to see with your own eyes at a flower show.

Deutzia × elegantissima

If you have a large garden, grow it in groups, if you have a small garden, grow it as a single shrub, but grow it you must. *Deutzia × elegantissima* is hardy, tidy, exquisite in flower, pleasant at all other seasons, grows in any soil, and asks nothing but a sunny place and an annual pruning.

It is a dense, upright, deciduous shrub 4 to 5 feet (1.2 to 1.5 m) tall which arches over in early summer, when every young shoot is loaded with clusters of small, rosy pink, starlike flowers, and *elegantissima* is the *mot juste*. In summer, it is covered with narrow green leaves until autumn, when the leaves fall to reveal a warm brown thicket which is an asset to the winter scene.

Prune the shrub thoroughly after flowering (this will take time), shortening every flowering shoot and cutting down some of the stems in the centre of the bush as low as you can reach.

Growth is too dense for underplanting, but I like to have white tulips and red *Anemone × fulgens* planted nearby to make a show before the *Deutzia* is ready.

Deutzia × elegantissima

In early summer the young shoots of *Deutzia × elegantissima* are crowded with apple-blossom pink buds that open to pale pink, starlike flowers. This deciduous shrub grows to about 5 feet (1.5 m).

Elaeagnus pungens 'Maculata' is a useful dense shrub, the yellow splash on the glossy leaves being particularly conspicuous in winter. Specimens rarely exceed 12 feet (3.6 m) in height and spread.

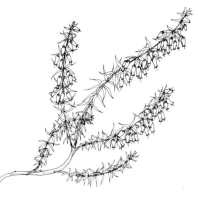

Erica carnea

Elaeagnus pungens 'Maculata'

W.J. Bean, author of the classic work on trees and shrubs, describes this shrub as 'the most striking of all variegated evergreens', and as its leaf colour is most brilliant in the winter, it has a strong claim to a place in every garden. The leaves are large, oval, glossy and bright green with a bright yellow splash down the middle.

This elaeagnus is very slow-growing, and though it is said to grow up to 15 feet (4.5 m), I have not seen it so tall, but it is a dense shrub, and even a young specimen makes its mark in a shrub border or in a sunny corner. It grows in any soil, does well in towns, shaping itself felicitously against a wall, and I have found it fully hardy. If any of the young shoots revert to bearing plain green leaves without the variegation, cut them out.

If *Helleborus foetidus* is planted at the foot of the shrub, there will be a cheerful late-winter picture of pale, dark and bright shades of green with yellow. Sprigs can be cut for the house, giving substance to a vase of winter jasmine or forsythia.

Erica carnea

I always think of heathers as somewhat gloomy flowers (I was reared on Thomas Hardy's novels of Egdon Heath), but they are beloved by so many gardeners that I am learning to see them with new eyes.

Heathers are evergreen sub-shrubs, many of which are calcifuge. But *E. carnea* is a lime-tolerant species, hardy and

winter-flowering, usually grown either in the rock garden, or as a thick, mat-forming ground-cover for larger beds or banks. It likes full sun. The bell-shaped flowers, white or pink, grow in thick pendant clusters, and the plants spread sideways to as much as 4 feet (1.2 m), so that they should be planted at intervals of 2 feet (60 cm) to make a quick, thick

carpet. Keep them weeded until they have formed their network of roots.

E. carnea comes in white and several shades of pink and red, and these can be grouped to make a tapestry if you have enough space. If you are confined to a single variety, I suggest the large-flowered 'Springwood White' to catch the pale winter sunlight. A prostrate juniper, like *J. horizontalis*, would make a striking contrast, but the dwarf pyramidal conifers, like exclamation marks, which are commonly used with heathers, are too Disneyland for me.

Clip heathers over after flowering, which, apart from the initial weeding, is all the attention they should need.

Many of the heaths and heathers will not tolerate lime but *Erica carnea* will even grow on chalky soils. This hardy species, which forms mounds 12 inches (30 cm) high, has pink or white flowers in winter.

The sulphur-yellow heads of *Euphorbia polychroma* make a bold splash in spring. This hardy evergreen sub-shrub forms dense cushions about 18 inches (45 cm) high and is attractive at all seasons.

Euphorbia polychroma

This sturdy sub-shrub is a perfect cushion plant for the front of a mixed border or shrub bed. It is always handsome, being evergreen and prolific of sulphur-yellow flowers on red stalks in spring. When the brilliant flowers have faded, they do not drop, but turn first green and later tawny red, adding colour to the garden in autumn; there is no need to cut them down until mid-winter. (What look like yellow petals are, technically, bracts, but this is immaterial to the non-botanical gardener.) The plant is hardy, reliable, and a weed-suppressor. It is sometimes listed as *E. epithymoides*.

There is a strong case for having cushion plants in the front of a bed, for they always look neat and save a lot of weeding, and the rounded shapes of sedum, alchemilla, epimedium and this

Euphorbia polychroma

euphorbia make a substantial foreground to the spires of summer perennials which will follow. Large adjoining clumps of *E. polychroma* and one of the epimediums, planted 3 feet (90 cm) apart, would give some pleasant russet foliage in autumn, for the narrow euphorbia leaves turn red and those of the epimedium bronze.

Forsythia × intermedia 'Specatabilis' is densely covered with bright yellow flowers in mid-spring. This deciduous shrub, which grows to 8 feet (2.4 m), is a dull plant after flowering but worth growing just for cutting.

Forsythia × intermedia 'Spectabilis'

I confess that I grow this tall shrub chiefly for its cutting value, for it is ungainly in shape and uninteresting after flowering. But it is so satisfying cutting long stems in tight bud six or seven weeks before flowering, when the weather is drear, and watching the bright yellow flowers come out slowly in a warm room, that I am glad to have a big specimen with whole branches to spare. 'Lynwood' is a variety with particularly large flowers.

Forsythia is hardy and deciduous, the

Forsythia × intermedia 'Spectabilis'

flowers coming out on pale brown, brittle branches before the oval leaves. It is a fast grower in any soil, and needs little attention. If you have cut it heavily for the house, it will not need pruning; otherwise shorten the old stems immediately after flowering, and cut one or two branches to the ground to encourage fresh growth.

I think forsythia looks better on a shrubby bank than against the house – it is particularly unfortunate against red brick. But among dark-leaved ever-greens, like *Elaeagnus × ebbingei*, it can make a fine sunny splash in spring.

Fritillaria imperialis

The crown imperial is a plant with a rare aura of grandeur. John Parkinson gave it the first place in his great book, *The Earthly Paradise*, in 1629 'for its stately beautifulness', and Vita Sackville-West of Sissinghurst reverenced its 'stiff Gothic-looking flowers'. Trekking through the

The crown imperial, *Fritillaria imperialis*, is a stately spring-flowering bulb with a head of hanging orange or yellow flowers on a stem up to 3 feet (90 cm) high, topped with a tuft of leaves.

wilds of Persia with tents and ponies in 1927, her greatest moment was when she reached a gorge carpeted with this fritillary and could pick it in armfuls. Though its natural scenery is theatrical, the mountains of Iran and Afghanistan, it condescends to associate well with simpler garden plants and has for centuries been grown in cottage gardens.

Fritillaria imperialis

A tall, stiff, bulbous plant up to 3 feet (90 cm) high, it is crowned with a circlet of hanging orange or yellow bells topped with a tuft of leaves like a pineapple. If you lift the bells you will find drops of nectar glistening inside. It flowers in spring, and the bulbs are best planted in clumps in a sunny border with a low ground cover at their base so that the strong stalks are not hidden – perhaps dog violets or *Geranium sanguineum*, which flowers later but will surround the lilies with small, fresh green leaves. They like a rich, well-drained soil and are happy with lime. Their only vice is a habit of coming up blind, which usually means a poverty of soil, and if this persists it is best to lift the bulbs and move them to another, well-manured spot, planting in holes three times the depth of the bulb. Some experts recommend planting the bulbs on their sides to keep water out, for the bulbs are hollow, but, even in the wild, a proportion will fail to flower.

Although they look so strange, many fritillaries are happy in the garden, and if you have a damp, grassy place it should suit the snake's-head fritillary, *F. meleagris*, with purple-and-white checkered bells, or white bells tinged with green. As a child, I used to pick them wild in the Loddon valley, the farmer charging three-pence for a large bunch – a forbidden treat today.

Gaillardia × *grandiflora*

In high summer there is an outburst of composite daisy flowers which take their hot colouring from the sun. Some think their brightness is fitting for the time of year, others find them gaudy, but the gardener cannot ignore them, or he would be short of flowers until the pink and blue revivals of autumn.

Among the finest of the big ray-flowered daisies is *Gaillardia* × *grandiflora*, a hardy perennial from North America, best chosen from several handsome hybrids in sunset colours, like 'Wirral Flame', a deep red with petals tipped with gold, or the orange 'Mandarin'. They are quite tall plants, 30 inches (75 cm) high in some varieties, and tend to flop without support. They flower for some three months and cut well.

With what colours will you plant them? Some gardeners like to soften the blaze of orange and yellow with blue flowers, like Michaelmas daisies or *Eryngium* × *oliverianum*, a metallic blue sea holly.

Gaillardia × *grandiflora*

Others go the whole hog and make a fiery garden with red, orange and gold plants, like *Crocosmia, Lychnis*, red hot pokers, achilleas, and shrubby hypericums. This was the theme of Harold Nicolson's Cottage Garden at Sissinghurst, the flamboyant colours being set off by the sombre green of Irish yews. But even in this dark background there was colour, for a climbing nasturtium, *Tropaeolum speciosum*, threaded its way up the yews, here and there darting out a scarlet tongue.

Gaillardia likes light, well-drained soil and full sun, and should be planted in clumps 18 inches (45 cm) apart.

Gaillardia × *grandiflora* is one of the bright daisy flowers of mid-summer. This hardy perennial, most forms of which grow about 30 inches (75 cm) high, may need some support but it has a long flowering season.

Galega officinalis 'Lady Wilson' is a good form of a hardy perennial vetch, with pea flowers combining light and dark shades of mauve. This is a plant for the middle or back of the border, growing to 3 feet (90 cm).

Geranium psilostemon

Even if it did not have spectacular flowers, this tall cranesbill would be worth growing for the series of changing leaf pictures which it presents over four months of the year. In spring, scarlet shoots start to push through the soil. By mid-summer they have burst into a mound of palmate green leaves. In autumn they often turn red and orange. The flowers join them in mid-summer, coming out in masses on tall branching stems, flat, round flowers of brilliant magenta with black centres. A very eye-catching plant indeed.

A hardy perennial, *G. psilostemon* grows in any good well-drained soil, and can be divided every two or three years to provide new plants, though it will also seed itself about the garden. It needs a little support – twiggy sticks if available,

'Bressingham Flair' is a particularly good form of a cranesbill, *Geranium psilostemon*. The mound of palmate green foliage, up to 30 inches (75 cm) high, is as valuable as the summer display of vivid flowers.

Galega officinalis

This tall and graceful vetch, commonly called goat's-rue, is a plant I would like to see in the wild, in its native haunts of the Balkans and Asia Minor. It does not look like a garden plant, yet visitors to my garden have so often asked for a piece that one year I found I had parted with my last root and had to ask for some back. It is an appealing plant for the middle or back of a border, a hardy perennial about 3 feet (90 cm) high with beautiful, fresh green, pinnate leaves with many spikes of mauve sweet-pea flowers springing from the axils. Galegas flower for about two months in mid-summer, and will produce more leaves and a few more flowers if you cut them down when faded. They need a little support, but not much; a single cane is enough.

There are several varieties in shades of mauve, a mauve-and-white bi-colour,

Galega officinalis

'Lady Wilson', and a white one, 'Alba'.

This plant is too modest to be planted with the more showy summer perennials, and I prefer it with roses, or perhaps with white Shasta daisies, or with foliage plants. Plant it in well-drained soil in sun, perhaps a group of three plants, 2 feet (60 cm) apart.

Geranium psilostemon

The unusual spidery flowers of the Chinese witch hazel, *Hamamelis mollis*, are lemon-yellow in the form 'Pallida'. These witch hazels have a height and spread of about 8 feet (2.4 m) and their leaves colour well in autumn.

otherwise the stems can be loosely tied to a single cane which will be hidden by foliage. One plant will make its mark if your space is restricted, but in a mixed border it is worth planting a group of three or five plants 2 feet (60 cm) apart, and giving considerable thought to its companions. I like it particularly in front of hybrid musk roses, perhaps a large shrub of the peach-pink, double rose 'Cornelia', or the creamy, semi-double 'Penelope', both generous with their clusters of

summer flowers. In the foreground, the white daisy flowers and creeping silver foliage of *Anthemis cupaniana* would look cool and refreshing.

This geranium is a staple plant in such famous red-and-purple borders as those at Hidcote Manor and Sissinghurst, along with purple delphiniums and campanulas, red *Lychnis*, fuchsias, *Lobelia cardinalis*, clematis, heliotrope, and many other plants of imperial splendour.

Hamamelis mollis

The Chinese witch hazel is a quite startling shrub to meet on a winter's day. When most of the garden has gone to sleep here is a tall, angular, twiggy plant very much alive and apparently covered with large yellow spiders. If the day is fine, these curious flowers will throw out a rich, sweet scent to a considerable distance.

Hamamelis is deciduous, fully hardy, likes full sun and a rich, lime-free soil, and is a particularly good town plant. Its flowering time varies with the weather, but usually starts in mid-winter and lasts for several weeks. The large, rough

leaves appear after the flowers are over and in autumn turn golden yellow. The bush grows to 8 feet (2.4 m) or more in height, with the same width across the crown of the bush.

The colour of *H. mollis* is a deep, heavy yellow, like the yellow of gorse, but the variety 'Pallida' is more attractive, with lemon-yellow flowers stained with wine-red in the centre. Plant it a few feet away from the house among low evergreens, like box or skimmia, and you have a shapely composition to enjoy through the windows in the darkest months.

Hamamelis mollis 'Pallida'

Hebe hybrids

I find hebes difficult to place in my garden, for visual, not practical reasons, because it always seems to me that plants from the antipodes, however beautiful, can look uneasy in the English scene, especially in downland. Yet hebes are exquisite in the right surroundings, and are now so popular in Britain that a Hebe Society was formed in 1985.

Once classed as veronicas, they are a large genus, nearly all exclusive to New Zealand, where some grow by the sea, others in river valleys or on mountain heights. All are evergreen. The species are mostly tender, but there are many fine garden hybrids which are robust in Britain, especially by the sea or in the shelter of a building. 'Midsummer Beauty' is exceptionally reliable, a rounded shrub

Hebe 'Alicia Amherst'

smothered with spikes of blue flowers from mid-summer almost into winter. The leaves are narrow and willow-like. 'Alicia Amherst' is another strong cultivar with larger blue flowers and broader

leaves, and 'Gauntlettii' is a pink-flowered variety. The colour range extends from white to magenta and dark purple.

Hebes will grow in any well-drained soil, are lime-tolerant and like full sun. Specialists recommend deep planting, with several buds below the soil, so that the plant will shoot again if damaged by frost. The use of a winter mulch will also give valuable protection.

A group of hebes, planted 3 to 4 feet (90 to 120 cm) apart, would make appropriate neighbours for the tall, architectural spikes of *Phormium tenax*, another New Zealander, which is hardy in all but the coldest places.

Heliopsis scabra

Like it or not, the plants of the family Compositae dominate the late summer garden. 'The hosts of Helianthus and Heliopsis, with the Michaelmas Daisies, form the battalions of Autumn', wrote E. A. Bowles, author of the classic *My Garden* trilogy. To ignore these hardy perennials is to have virtually no flowers in the summer-into-autumn period, and it is better to welcome them and mass them together in a blaze of red and gold, as in a Victorian cottage garden. *Heliopsis*,

Heliopsis scabra

golden rod, rudbeckia, softened by Michaelmas daisies, with poppies and red hot pokers from other plant families, make a robust response to those discreet gardeners who settle at this time of year for late roses and foliage plants.

The hebes are evergreen shrubs that were formerly grouped with the veronicas. 'Midsummer Beauty' is a hybrid that grows to about 4 feet (1.2 m) high and has a long flowering season from mid-summer to autumn.

Heliopsis scabra, sometimes listed under *H. helianthoides,* is one of the best of the yellow composite plants, with single or double bright gold flowers, the fully double ones looking almost like giant zinnias. They are from 3 to 4 feet (90 to 120 cm) tall, need no staking, and can be cut for weeks on end. 'Golden Plume' is one of several good double varieties.

Plant 2 feet (60 cm) apart in groups in any garden soil, including quite dry soil.

'Golden Plume' is a good double form of *Heliopsis scabra,* one of the yellow composites that are so prominent in late summer. This species grows to about 4 feet (1.2 m) high but does not need staking.

Hemerocallis flava

Hemerocallis, or day lilies, are today being collected, hybridized, and exhibited with the passion which once inspired the tulipomaniacs of Holland or, a century later, the auricula fanciers in Britain. The modern fashion has been led by enthusiasts in the United States, but now day lilies are becoming highly popular in Britain, too. The lilies vary in their season of flowering, so that it is possible to have a succession from early summer right into the autumn.

Hemerocallis flava is an early flowering species of day lily, a group of hardy herbaceous perennials, now much hybridized and increasingly popular. The flower stems of this species are about 3 feet (90 cm) tall.

They are herbaceous perennials, very vigorous and easy to grow, with clusters of trumpet flowers at the top of tall stalks, opening one every day over several weeks. The handsome clumps of bright green, arching, grassy leaves make day lilies an important foliage plant.

Hemerocallis flava, the lemon day lily, also listed as *H. lilio-asphodelus,* is an

early-flowering species from the Far East which has been grown in Britain for four hundred years. Its yellow trumpet flowers on stalks 3 feet (90 cm) high are richly scented. *H. fulva,* another species with a long garden history, with orange flowers, starts to bloom three or four weeks later, after mid-summer. A few other species, and a wide range of hybrids, are available to the gardener.

Day lilies should be planted at least 18 inches (45 cm) apart and can be grown almost anywhere if the soil is good. They prefer sun, accept light shade, are excellent in town gardens, and can even be grown in grass if there is enough moisture. They should not be divided unless the flowers diminish in number, a sign of overcrowding.

The yellow day lilies look wonderful with delphiniums, or other blue flowers, and are good plants to take over when spring-flowering shrubs have bloomed and the beds need fresh colour.

Hemerocallis flava

Iris histrioides
'Major'

This beautiful little iris from Asia Minor flowers even earlier than *I. reticulata*, in the depth of winter. It is the deep madonna blue of Italian paintings, with gold and white markings on the falls, and is so hardy that it will come up undamaged through a carpet of snow. Its only drawback is that it has no scent, but if you can find a few early *I. reticulata* to pick with them you can cheat a little and have a scented bowl in the house.

Iris histrioides can be grown in the rock garden, or in sinks or pots, or it can be allowed to naturalize in a sunny corner, with snowdrops and aconites round about. It needs good drainage, preferably in light, limy soil, and to succeed in heavy soil should be grown in a raised bed, or at least with plenty of grit. Plant at random 2 to 3 inches (5 to 7.5 cm) deep.

The bulbous irises include some of the most exquisite flowers of winter and early spring. *Iris histrioides* 'Major', which is only about 4 inches (10 cm) high, will pierce snow to open its flowers.

Iris reticulata

This little bulb (named after the net-like coat of fibres which protects the bulb itself) is one of the best-loved of all irises, giving pleasure out of all proportion to its size – it is only a few inches tall. Its velvety blue flowers flecked with gold arrive in very early spring, and are heavily scented.

Iris reticulata

It is quite hardy and increases fast in well-drained, preferably alkaline soil – a few bulbs planted 3 inches (7.5 cm) deep and 4 inches (10 cm) apart in autumn will form an established colony in a year or two.

Being so small, do not let the irises get swamped in a large border. Perhaps you have a narrow bed by the house where they would be more conspicuous. They are also ideal for the rock garden, or for raised troughs, where they can be seen and sniffed near eye-level. Several varieties are available, ranging from light blue to dark purple.

After flowering, the leaves present a problem, for they grow very tall and grassy and are something of an eyesore,

Iris reticulata, despite its fragile appearance, is a hardy dwarf bulb that flowers in late winter or early spring. The scented flowers stand about 4 inches (10 cm) high but the leaves extend beyond them.

and must not, of course, be cut down. A light, non-strangulating ground-cover might be planted nearby, such as the pink-flowered *Geranium endressii*.

In her epic poem *The Land*, Vita Sackville-West honoured *I. reticulata* as one of the earliest flowers of the year.

> For no new flowers shall be born
> Save hellebore on Christmas morn,
> And bare gold jasmine on the wall,
> And violets, and soon the small
> Blue netted iris, like a cry
> Startling the sloth of February.

Kolkwitzia amabilis

This tall and lovely deciduous shrub needs quite a bit of space, perhaps in the centre of an island bed; it forms a thicket up to 12 feet (3.6 m) high, and nearly as much in width. It is one of the glorious shrubs from west China introduced early in this century by E.H. Wilson, known as

Kolkwitzia amabilis

'Chinese Wilson', the indomitable botanist-collector-explorer who visited China four times and is said to have introduced more than 1,200 species of trees and shrubs to the West. Gardeners in the United States, who have grown *Kolkwitzia amabilis* ever since its discovery, call it the 'beauty bush'.

Though the main stems of the shrub are upright, they arch over in early summer from the weight of the blossom – large clusters of small, pink, bell-shaped flowers with yellow throats, best in the variety 'Rosea'. In autumn the pointed oval leaves turn a rich scarlet, making a

Kolkwitzia amabilis, the beauty bush, can grow to 12 feet (3.6 m) and almost as much across. The flowers in late spring and early summer are its main beauty but the foliage colours well in autumn.

Lathyrus odoratus

fine second burst of colour.

A native of rocky places and high mountains, *Kolkwitzia* is very hardy and reliable; it needs full sun, and will grow in any soil, being especially vigorous on chalk. After flowering, prune it in the same way as *Deutzia*. Put it with naturalized plants round about (nothing too formal) such as hellebores, Japanese anemones and campanulas.

Lathyrus odoratus

The sweet-pea is too well known to need description. All one can usefully do is to discuss various ways of growing this marvellous hardy annual.

I used, years ago, to sow frilled Spencer sweet-peas in the open ground in spring, in a heavily manured place in full sun, and never failed to revel in weeks of flowers from mid-summer onward. I grew them up peasticks cottage fashion – I still like them best this way, and grow hazel bushes to provide the sticks – and I cut and deadheaded them religiously, never allowing a seed pod to weaken the plants. In dry weather I gave them a thin mulch of grass mowings, not too fresh and steamy. This is an amateur's method, and serious gardeners who want larger and finer flowers grow sweet-peas up tall canes, pinching out all tendrils and tying in the shoots.

Today, sowing in the open ground (in Britain, at any rate) is a thing of the past, for our climate has changed so much, the spring getting ever colder and later, that one must sow seeds under glass and plant out later, or else buy plants. I like a mixture of pale 'sweet-pea' shades with one or two richer colours, like wine-coloured 'Beaujolais' or mauve-blue 'Noel Sutton'.

In addition to the Spencer sweet-peas, it is nice to sow a little group of the old grandiflora sweet-peas (that is, sweet-peas before the first large-flowered, frilled, modern sweet-peas were bred in 1899), which are smaller, but have a stronger scent. Most seedsmen sell these in mixed packets, but good named varieties, if you can find them, are 'Matucana', a maroon and violet bi-colour, and 'Sicilian Pink', which is cyclamen-pink and white.

One deplorable modern heresy is the dwarfing of sweet-peas, a novelty damned by splendid old Miss Jekyll, who called them 'little dwarf monstrosities'.

The sweet-pea, *Lathyrus odoratus*, is a hardy annual climber that can grow to 10 feet (3 m). The modern varieties have large, scented flowers in a wide range of colours. Even more fragrant are the old Grandiflora sweet-peas.

She felt that the beautiful flowers should be seen on a level with the eye. As the stunted sweet-peas 'require a little support', which is a euphemism for staking, I see no point in them.

Lavatera trimestris

This is one of the best hardy annuals for the sunny garden, filling in the gap when the peonies and early perennials are over and the late perennials are not yet in their prime. A bushy plant up to 3 feet (90 cm) high, it is covered with trumpet flowers for many weeks from midsummer. One of the best varieties is 'Loveliness', with satiny rose-pink flowers; 'Silver Cup' is pink with a silver gleam; 'Mont Blanc', a shorter plant with pure white flowers, is perhaps the best of all.

The pink ones need careful placing.

Lavatera trimestris 'Mont Blanc' is one of the best of the hardy annual mallows and slightly shorter than most of the pink-flowered varieties, which can make bushy plants up to 3 feet (90 cm) high.

They look well among peony foliage with shrub roses in the background, and there might be a group of purple-leaved plants in front, such as *Sedum maximum* 'Atropurpureum', or the silver-leaved *Stachys olympica*. Alternatively, sow them among evergreen shrubs such as *Viburnum* × *burkwoodii* to cheer them up after they have flowered.

The seeds are best sown in spring where they are to flower, and they are nice large seeds, so you can see what you are doing. Any garden soil suits them. Thin them when the seedlings are large enough, and water if necessary. Deadhead the plants from time to time if you have the patience, but leave a few seedheads to sow themselves for an early crop next year.

Lavatera trimestris

Lilium regale

Lilium regale has such an exotic beauty that it is difficult to believe that it is one of the easiest lilies to grow. Admiring its stately height, marvelling at its pure white, trumpet flowers with yellow in the throat and wine-red shading on the back of the petals, and drinking in its overpowering scent, you would imagine that this bulb needed infinite cosseting. In fact, it is fully hardy, happy in any well-drained soil, whether acid or alkaline, dislikes rich food, and in most gardens increases fast. It flowers soon after mid-summer. All it asks is sun and the backing of a wall or shrubs to protect it from wind. I give it pride of place over the equally beautiful madonna lily, *L. candidum*, which has been known to civilization for thousands of years, because the madonna lily is erratic, and may die out in a garden for no obvious reason.

The bulbs of *L. regale* should be planted fairly deeply, about 8 inches (20 cm) below the surface, 12 inches (30 cm) apart, and it takes at least six to make a substantial group. If there is no protecting wall, then a shrub with dark, glossy leaves, like *Viburnum* × *burkwoodii*, makes an

excellent background, and I think that modest, uncompetitive plants with soft blue flowers make the best companions. Three plants of *Nepeta* 'Six Hills Giant', a large herbaceous plant some 3 feet (90 cm) in height and spread, would make a

Lilium regale

The most spectacular of the summer-
flowering bulbs are the lilies and
the regal lily, *Lilium regale*, is one
of the easiest. Its trumpet flowers are
carried on stems up to 6 feet (1.8m)
tall and are richly scented.

semi-circle in front of a group of *L. regale*,
and would continue in flower when the
lilies were over.

The origin of *L. regale* is romantic, for
as far as is known it grows wild in only
one place in the world, in a river valley in
remotest north-west China. Here it was
discovered growing in tens of thousands
in 1903 by the greatest of all plant
collectors, E.H. Wilson.

Limnanthes douglasii

One of the most charming of all cottage
plants, this hardy annual came to us from
North America, where it is known as
meadow foam, in 1833. Delicately
scented and beloved by bees, it was
widely grown by Victorian country-
women in their special 'bee gardens'.

Limnanthes is a dwarf plant with flowers like primroses, but white with yellow
centres (it is sometimes called poached-
egg flower), and fresh green, pinnate,
almost fernlike, leaves. It flowers in late
spring and seeds in perpetuity, so long as
you leave the plants for several weeks
after flowering for the seeds to ripen and
scatter. Any soil will suit it. It looks well in
the front of a sunny or lightly shaded
border with foliage plants behind.

Limnanthes is one of my favourite
flowers, but my pleasure is slightly tem-
pered by guilt when I think of its unhappy
discoverer, the lonely Scotsman, David
Douglas, who collected many plants,
especially conifers, in the wilds of western
North America in the early nineteenth
century. Douglas was not a joyous collector, but was always in difficulties, losing his
seeds in flooding rivers, nearly dying of
starvation, or being attacked by hostile
Indians, and at the early age of thirty-five
he was killed by falling into a wild bullpit in
Hawaii. But at least his name will always
be associated with a plant which is as
exquisite to look at as it is easy to grow.

The poached-egg flower, *Limnanthes douglasii* is a hardy annual that self-seeds
freely. The fresh green leaves are almost smothered in spring by the flowers,
forming a dazzling mat about 6 inches (15 cm) high.

Many magnolias are slow to reach flowering age. *Magnolia stellata*, which grows to about 12 feet (3.6m), is an outstanding deciduous species that is slow-growing but flowers when young, and will tolerate lime.

Magnolia stellata

This is one of the most versatile of magnolias, and certainly the best for small gardens. It is a hardy and compact deciduous shrub which grows slowly but flowers when young, producing masses of pure white, scented blossom reliably every spring. The flowers, which appear on bare branches, are quite unlike those of the cup-shaped magnolias, and have many ribbon-like petals, so that the bush really does look starry in its season.

Magnolia stellata grows to about 12 feet (3.6 m), looking dramatic as a specimen shrub in a lawn, but it could also take its place among other shrubs, or by the house. To add to its other virtues, it is lime-tolerant, though it wants good soil, and on chalk soils should be dressed with peat. There is a pinkish variety called 'Rosea' but I prefer the purity of the white-flowered species. Some blue bulbs

round about would be good companions; I suggest blue anemones (*A. blanda* or *A. nemorosa* 'Robinsoniana', a blue form of wood anemone) or grape hyacinths, but in some gardens these last seed too freely and become a troublesome weed.

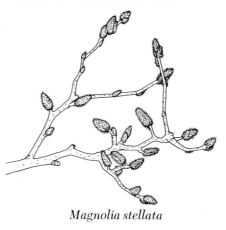

Magnolia stellata

Narcissus cyclamineus

Every reader of this book will have grown or known many different daffodils. Even the gardening beginner has surely at some time nurtured a 'Paper White' narcissus in a pot. Some have seen our native daffodil, *Narcissus pseudo-narcissus*, by the lakes in the Wordsworth country, and all have bought daffodils in green bud in winter and watched them slowly open to cheer up the room.

There are so many daffodils being grown today — literally thousands of varieties — that it is impossible to treat them in depth in a book of this size.

All I can do in my space is to choose my favourite *kind* of narcissus, which is known unromantically as the 'Cyclamineus Division', that is, a group of narcissi with laid-back petals, like those of a cyclamen, round a longish, trumpet-

Narcissus cyclamineus, a dwarf species of daffodil, is a parent of many hybrids with petals swept back from the trumpet. 'March Sunshine', which grows to about 12 inches (30cm), shows the grace of this species.

shaped cup. On the small side, these narcissi have a grace denied to the large-flowered giants, and they lend themselves well to naturalizing, which is what daffodils were born for. Two of the loveliest of this kind are 'February Gold' and 'Dove Wings'. The former has a frilled golden trumpet and reflexed petals of the same colour, and flowers early. 'Dove Wings' looks gentle and demure with a pale lemon cup and white petals.

Narcissus cyclamineus

Both are 12 inches (30 cm) tall. Another interesting variety in the same group, also early and good for naturalizing, is 'Peeping Tom', with an exceptionally long, narrow golden trumpet.

There are also some tiny cyclamineus narcissi for the rock garden or for pots and window-boxes in a town garden, of which 'Tête-à-Tête' is irresistible, but I will write about this on page 150.

For naturalizing, plant daffodils in woodland soil or in grass in sun or light shade in holes three times the depth of the bulb, and I know no better way of achieving a random look than that told me by an old countryman when I was a child: 'Throw them in the air and plant them where they fall.'

Nepeta
'Six Hills Giant'

The catmints are some of the most harmonious of plants against brick and stone, softening the hardness with their gentle texture and colouring. Of these herbaceous perennials, 'Six Hills Giant' is a

The catmints are herbaceous perennials that will produce a second crop of foliage and flowers if cut back after the first flowering. *Nepeta* 'Six Hills Giant' will grow to 30 inches (75 cm) and is a good mixer.

particularly robust variety, about 30 inches (75 cm) tall, with grey-green aromatic leaves and lavender-blue, labiate flowers that continue all through the summer. It is a fine middle border plant, with the virtue of being self-supporting.

A group of five plants, placed 2 feet (60 cm) apart, would blend with other herbaceous perennials or with shrub roses. A combination that I have particularly admired is its soft blue flowers against the apricot clusters of the musk rose 'Buff Beauty'.

Nepeta x *faassenii*, which grows to about 12 inches (30 cm), is smaller in all its parts and looks well drooping down over a wall or across a path. As well as its merits for the front of a border, the plant is a good filler for odd corners.

Nepetas can be clipped after the first blooming, but the second flush of stalks and flowers should be left uncut through the winter to protect the heart of the plant from frost.

Nepeta 'Six Hills Giant'

Oenothera missouriensis

This prostrate perennial evening primrose is becoming increasingly popular, and rightly so. A first-rate introduction from the United States, it has astonishingly large and conspicuous flowers for its size, lemon-yellow trumpets up to 4 inches (10 cm) across on diminutive stalks rising from a mat of long, narrow, pointed leaves. It flowers for many weeks through the summer and is a fine plant for the front of a sunny border, or for a rock garden. Space the plants 18 inches (45 cm) apart in any good garden soil.

In the border, you need at least five plants to make a show, and they look particularly well illuminating plants of dusky blue. Try a patch in front of purple-leaved sage (*Salvia officinalis* 'Purpurascens'), or *Salvia* × *superba*, with spires of purple-blue labiate flowers which provide a contrast of form as well as colour. The area covered by the

Oenothera missouriensis

Oenothera should be labelled in late autumn, for the plant dies down to the last scrap of leaf and can easily be forked over and lost.

Gardeners who grow *Oenothera missouriensis* differ in their observation of its flowering timetable. Some say it is a true evening primrose, others that it flowers all day. I myself have seen it in many gardens fully open at noon.

Oenothera missouriensis, a perennial evening primrose, is suitable for the border or the rock garden. The trailing stems carry a long succession of lemon-yellow flowers, which stand about 6 inches (15 cm) high.

Paeonia mlokosewitschii

Some gardeners complain that peonies have too short a period of beauty to justify their space, especially in a small garden, but peony 'mlok' cannot be so accused. Flowering in mid-spring, when the weather is still cool or cold, you should be able to enjoy its lemon-yellow single flowers (lemon with a hint of green)

Paeonia mlokosewitschii is a herbaceous species up to 2 feet (60 cm) tall that flowers in mid-spring. As well as having lemon-yellow flowers of cool beauty, this peony has attractive foliage and unusual seed-pods.

for three weeks. Each flower has a large boss of deeper yellow stamens.

But 'mlok' is lovely both before and after flowering. A herbaceous perennial, its crimson shoots start to push through the soil in winter, one of the first signs of hope on the way. The leaves are a charming soft blue-green all through spring and summer, and there are curious seed-pods in autumn, which split to reveal a double row of large red and black seeds.

If you have bought plants, put them in 3 feet (90 cm) apart in manured soil just below the surface, in sun or dappled shade, allowing space for as large a patch as you can spare. If you are a patient gardener, and can wait five years for flowers, sow seeds in a box and leave it outside against a north wall until shoots appear, which may take two years. Then plant them in their final quarters and never disturb them, but add manure round the plants, *not* on the shoots, every autumn.

My own patch is planted in a bed

under an apple tree with blue *Clematis macropetala* climbing into its branches, and the two come out together.

Paeonia officinalis 'Rubra Plena'

'No flower that I know so faire, great and double' wrote John Parkinson of the crimson cottage peony in 1629 in his classic work *The Earthly Paradise*, and I can do no better than quote his admiring words. Perhaps it is childish of me to choose it as a favourite plant when there are available so many glorious modern hybrids, of Chinese rather than European origin, but its history as an English garden plant is so old that I am much attached to it. Though its flowering season is short, the huge, rich green, deep-cut leaves make some of the best foliage in the garden, and as the flower buds come out in succession, not all at once, they should

The double form of the European herbaceous peony, *Paeonia officinalis* 'Rubra Plena', makes a sturdy clump about 2 feet (60 cm) tall, the deeply cut foliage setting off the large heads of crimson flowers.

give you a month's pleasure. They are perfect for cutting, perhaps just three or four stems, leaves and all, with some white lilac.

They make large plants 2 feet (60 cm) tall, flowering in late spring, and grow best in rich, well-drained soil, mulched annually with manure. They love lime, even chalk. They are mainly plants for the sun, but will tolerate light shade, in which case the flowers will last longer.

The scented Chinese peonies are taller and flower later, in early summer, and there is a vast range of hybrids available in red, pink, cream or white. One of the finest is the double 'Lady Alexandra Duff', a pure, sweet pink seen at its luscious best with shrub roses in the forecourt of the Elizabethan garden at Cranborne Manor, in Dorset.

Plant peonies in autumn 3 feet (90 cm) apart with plenty of manure, and do not plant deep. If undisturbed they will last for a lifetime.

Paeonia officinalis 'Rubra Plena'

Philadelphus 'Beauclerk'

The beautiful mock orange is to me the very essence of mid-summer, casting its heavy scent far into the garden. You must give the shrub generous space, for it grows about 6 feet (1.8 m) tall and wide, and in its season every branch is loaded with clusters of very large, flat, four-petalled white flowers with yellow stamens. (Most catalogues say that it is flushed with pink in the centre, but mine is pure white.) It cries aloud to be planted with old-fashioned roses, especially the bourbons, like 'Madame Isaac Pereire' or 'Gypsy Boy', both being crimson and double.

A rival *Philadelphus* in my affections is the taller 'Belle Etoile', with cup-shaped single flowers stained with purple in the centre. The scent is equally strong, but

Philadelphus 'Belle Etoile'

the bush is a little ungainly in shape, and the flowers are slightly smaller.

Both varieties are hardy and extremely easy to grow in any soil in a sunny place. They are excellent for cutting, especially with roses. As soon as flowering is over, cut off the spent branches, but leave the young upright shoots which will flower next year. They are shrubs which never fail you.

Philadelphus 'Beauclerk' is one of the finest hybrid mock oranges, with richly scented flowers in mid-summer. This deciduous shrub grows to about 6 feet (1.8 m) high and almost as wide.

The pasque flower, *Pulsatilla vulgaris*, is a herbaceous perennial that is suitable for the border or the rock garden. The flowers stand about 12 inches (30 cm) high and are followed by fluffy seedheads.

Pulsatilla vulgaris

This glorious member of the anemone family, called the pasque-flower, grows wild on the chalk downs near my cottage which means, according to legend, that Danish blood was spilt there centuries ago. In the garden, it is usually grown as a rock plant, but is just as appropriate in the foreground of any sunny corner. Strangely enough, though a native of downland, it

Pulsatilla vulgaris

does not seem to thrive if planted in turf.

The flowers bloom in Britain at Pasque or Easter time, in years when this movable feast falls late. They are large, of a deep violet colour with bright yellow stamens. The leaves and stalks are covered with silky hairs, and fluffy seedheads follow the flowers. There are garden varieties available in wine-red and white.

Plant *Pulsatilla* in well-drained soil, preferably limy, the plants 10 inches (25 cm) apart – they will form good clumps if left undisturbed. If a companion is wanted for the violet species, I cannot imagine anything better than white. *Arabis caucasica* would be delightful, though it can be invasive, or perhaps a mound of the dwarf shrub *Iberis sempervirens*, which is neatness itself.

ROSE SPECIES AND CULTIVARS

Roses are so desirable that no garden without them is worthy of the name. Every rose, from the innocent species with single flowers to the luscious centifolias, contributes a romantic quality to a garden which no other family of plants can match. But one cannot pretend that roses are particularly easy to grow. They want loving cultivation and protection against the pests and diseases to which many are prone. All roses like rich but well-drained soil and a sunny position; some need regular feeding, others need training, most need pruning, and some require regular spraying if attacked by enemies. They are *not* trouble-free.

When choosing roses it is wise not to be bewitched by the lovely old names into choosing varieties which are for the historian rather than for the working gardener, but to consider the vigour of each rose, the kind of soil and position you can offer it, and the length of its flowering season. In general, rose species will be strong and healthy, though the flowering season will be short, and shrub roses will make the best all-round garden plants, especially the relatively modern ones. Shrub roses will grow in any good soil; they need minimal pruning; and they

blend beautifully with other plants, especially in a mixed border. At the other end of the scale are the hybrid teas, which are labour-intensive. They need rich soil which is not too alkaline, hard pruning in spring, regular feeding and spraying, and they look best in special rosebeds of their own – but the blooms are superb.

In between come the climbers and ramblers and the floribunda, or cluster, roses. When choosing climbers, pick varieties recommended for vigour and two flowering seasons, and if you are bad on ladders, consider a pillar rose rather than a giant rambler. Floribundas are less fussy than hybrid teas as to soil and need only light pruning, while the more graceful ones, like 'Iceberg', can be blended into a mixed planting.

Instructions for growing roses can be found in many rose books and, more succinctly, in rose catalogues. All I would suggest here is that you pay special attention to your roses when you plant. Dig the ground some weeks in advance, working in rotted manure or compost, and when you plant make a large hole so that the roots are not cramped, scatter in some bonemeal and peat, and plant firmly. And when the flowers die, deadhead thoroughly, a job which is sometimes neglected. An hour spent deadheading your roses will make the whole garden look fresh and flowery, and will encourage a succession of bloom.

Rosa 'Aloha'

I was predisposed to like 'Aloha' before I ever met it, for one of its parents is my old friend, that fantastic climber, 'The New Dawn'. But 'Aloha', bred in 1949, is a much smaller climber, growing to about 8 feet (2.4 m), and is the perfect rose for a pillar or fence or for the wall of a cottage. It is as nearly perpetual as a rose can be, starting to produce its large, double, deep pink, scented flowers in early summer, and continuing to bloom into autumn. The stems are strong so that the clusters cut well for the house, and the leaves are glossy and resistant to mildew.

'Aloha' is a modern climbing rose of short stature, which will grow to about 8 feet (2.4 m). It is reliably healthy, free-flowering and the double flowers are scented.

'Aloha' is often grown as a shrub rose, but is large and needs much space. On a wall or fence it makes a good backdrop for one or two bushes of dark green rosemary or, alternatively, for grey-leaved plants, like artemisia, santolina or lavender. It is one of the roses which will take light shade, and I have seen it growing strongly in London gardens.

Rosa
'Canary Bird'

This is always the first rose to flower in my garden, beating 'Frühlingsgold' by a week, and is therefore specially beloved, though its beauty of flower, leaf and form would place it high in my affections at any season. A large, arching bush about 7 feet (2.1 m) tall and wide, it has warm brown stems covered in bright yellow small single flowers in late spring. The leaves grow in fernlike sprays, and occasionally there are small black hips in late summer. Like so many of my favourite plants, it comes from north China, and (mere fancy, perhaps) I feel that Chinese plants have a recognizable look, the exquisite quality of Chinese art.

'Canary Bird' likes well-drained soil, preferably limy, and looks its best in a bank or border of shrubs, with a few foliage plants, like *Brunnera macrophylla*, at its feet. Critics will tell you that it may suddenly die, which one plant did with me, but after sixteen years of perfection, I did not complain, but replaced it.

Rosa 'Canary Bird'

Rosa glauca

One of the loveliest of all rose species, *Rosa glauca* or *R. rubrifolia*, a tall shrub with arching branches, is not only a graceful plant in itself, but makes perfect company for all manner of other plants. Though the light clusters of dog-rose flowers, pink with a white eye, have a doll's-house charm, their season is short, and the great quality of *R. glauca* is its long-lasting foliage. Blue-green ferny leaves, with a soft bloom on the surface, contrasting with red stalks and midribs, remain fresh from early summer until well into autumn; during all this period branches can be cut for the house, and new shoots will follow. An added interest

One of the earliest roses to flower is the modern shrub 'Canary Bird'. The single yellow flowers smother the arching stems of bushes that can have a height and spread of 7 feet (2.1 m). The ferny leaves are bluish green.

The chief beauty of *Rosa glauca*, which can grow to 7 feet (2.1 m), is the foliage, ferny and blue-green with contrasting red stems and ribs. There is often a good crop of hips that colour well in autumn.

is the bunches of red berries which appear in late summer.

The rose can be grown in sun or light shade, and a single specimen, or a group of three, in a border would make a telling background for a succession of white flowers – white double peonies, delphiniums, campanulas, phlox and many more. But it will also thrive in deeper shade under trees, when pink or white martagon lilies would be good companions. Personally, I find the foliage grows more luxuriantly in shade.

In many gardens, *R. glauca* seeds freely, and the seedlings are treasures to be

Rosa glauca

earmarked until they are large enough to transplant. They will, of course, be sucker-free, which is not always true of commercially bought plants if they are grafted on to brier.

Rosa 'Iceberg'

Perhaps the most famous of all modern roses (it was bred of hybrid musk parentage in 1958), 'Iceberg' is so tall and vigorous that it can, if you wish, be treated not as a floribunda but as a shrub rose, when it will have the virtue of perpetual flowering denied to the true shrubs. If you want this, prune it only lightly in spring, and it will grow to about 5 feet (1.5 m).

'Iceberg' has sprays of long white buds,

Rosa 'Iceberg'

tinged with pink, which open to a greenish white. The first flush of flowers is abundant and prolonged, there is then usually a slight pause, and then another flowering which is as good as the first.

The floribundas, or cluster-flowered bush roses, bloom freely over a long season. 'Iceberg', an outstanding example, has greenish-white flowers. It can make a shrub about 5 feet (1.5 m) tall but is often kept smaller.

The leaves are a pale fresh green.

'Iceberg' is much used in grey-green-and-white gardens with white herbaceous plants, turk's-cap lilies, pinks, lavender, hostas, clematis and box. Box or yew hedging is an essential background to a white garden, or the whole ghostly thing tends to float away into nothingness. 'Iceberg' is also lovely in a formal rosebed grown with the blueish-red 'Rosemary Rose', which has red foliage, so that both flowers and leaves provide a colour contrast. This rose is a modern floribunda, but has full, quartered flowers like a Victorian rose, and a rich scent.

Rosa
'Madame Isaac Pereire'

Choosing favourite roses is a daunting task, since every rose is a joy in its season, and one must look for some extra merit, besides beauty of flower, such as elegant

'Madame Isaac Pereire', a bourbon rose dating from 1880, is exceptionally fragrant growing to 7 feet (2.1 m) or more. There is an autumn flush after the main summer season.

foliage or a long flowering season. The bourbon rose 'Madame Isaac Pereire', dating back to 1880, but of undiminished vigour today, must come high in the hierarchy of shrub roses, for it is 'old-fashioned' in the best sense, the huge, light crimson blooms being quartered and double, and the scent sweet and strong, while the main flowering season, in mid-summer, has a follow-up in autumn.

It is described in Bean as 'one of the most perfect and large of all roses, from half-open flower to expanded bloom'.

I like it best grown as a shrub in a rose garden or mixed border, its height of 6 feet (1.8 m) being somewhat too low for a wall or pillar. I have also seen it in a large garden grown as a magnificent hedge. Like all roses, it needs plenty of organic food and judicious pruning; as well as cutting out dead wood in spring, cut an occasional tired-looking stem down to the ground. I do not find that the usual instructions for shrub roses – 'no pruning

Rosa 'Madame Isaac Pereire'

required' – work well in practice. After a very cold spring, the first blooms of this rose may be malformed, but the later blooms will be perfect.

I suggest underplanting 'Madame Isaac Pereire' with *Stachys olympica*, or some other silver plant, to soften the almost excessive brilliance of its colour.

Rosa moyesii

This is one of the most dramatic summer-flowering rose species, for the shrub is very tall and erect, up to 10 feet (3 m) high, and the single flowers which line the branches are blood-red. The ferny leaves, consisting of many leaflets, are a pleasure to the eye all through the summer, and the fruits which follow in late summer are large, scarlet and curiously shaped like miniature pitchers. It is a vigorous rose, given any good garden soil. It was introduced to the West from China in 1903 by E.H. Wilson, and named after a missionary, the Rev. J. Moyes.

Rosa moyesii 'Geranium' is a reasonably compact form of a species that can grow to 10 feet (3 m). There is a fine display of single blood-red flowers, and in autumn there are large orange hips.

Many of our best Chinese plants were collected at the turn of the century by missionaries, especially the French Jesuits, like Père Delavay and Père David, who botanized when they could spare time from converting the heathen. There are several cultivars of *R. moyesii*, of which 'Geranium', with scarlet flowers, is outstanding, smaller than the species, and more suitable for small gardens.

Rosa moyesii

Rosa moyesii is unusually vertical in growth, indeed almost gaunt, and needs careful underplanting with herbaceous flowers. *Alchemilla mollis* is, as always, perfect, or blue hardy geraniums, like 'Johnson's Blue', could run in and out among the rose's roots and stray towards the front of the border.

Rosa 'Nevada'

One of the most spectacular of modern shrub roses, 'Nevada' makes an arching bush up to 7 feet (2.1 m) tall and as much in width. It flowers for two months from early summer, when every branch is massed with large white single flowers with yellow stamens, the white petals faintly tinged with pink. The summer display being prodigal and prolonged, there is not much of a repeat flowering, though there are occasional new blooms in early autumn.

'Nevada' needs a place at the back of a wide bed and looks best with striking groups of herbaceous plants in front. I have seen it as a background to clumps of red and orange flowers – Chinese peonies and oriental poppies (which coincide with the first weeks of 'Nevada'), followed by *Geranium psilostemon*, *Lychnis chalcedonica* and day lilies. In the foreground of this planting there was a group of *Allium albopilosum*, with large globular heads of metallic purplish starry flowers in mid-summer. This is a complicated planting in a large, well-tended garden; it would be simpler to use 'Nevada' as a backdrop for blue bearded irises.

Like most shrub roses, 'Nevada' needs little pruning, but plenty of good food.

Rosa 'Papa Meilland'

Hybrid tea roses do not do well on my light soil, but if I could grow them I would go all out for sumptuous colour and smell. 'Papa Meilland' is a classic red rose with velvety crimson flowers and an over-

The hybrid teas, or large-flowered bush roses, have shapely flowers, conical in bud and bowl-shaped when open. 'Papa Meilland' has sumptuous flowers with a rich scent but it can be disease prone.

The modern shrub rose 'Nevada' makes a large bush, up to 7 feet (2.1 m) high and across, that flowers profusely for almost two months in summer. Later, there are occasional flowers until autumn.

powering scent. The shapely flowers come lavishly through the summer, and are held on strong necks, an asset if you want impressive roses for cutting.

One or two hybrid teas of special vigour will grow well enough on light soil if fed generously, of which I can report well of 'Madame Butterfly', with clusters of shell-pink flowers flushed with gold at the centre, blueish leaves and a soft, sweet scent, but in general I confine myself to shrub roses and floribundas.

All hybrid teas prefer a rich soil and need a hard pruning in spring. Where to place them in the garden is a more difficult matter, for the growth is too stiff for an informal setting and they do not look at ease in a mixed border. I like them best grown in their own rosebeds in the traditional head gardener's way, where one can admire their sheer magnificence. Pansies, again a time-honoured choice, make a neat and appropriate underplanting.

Rosa rugosa 'Frau Dagmar Hastrup'

Every garden should have some rugosa roses, for they make tall, bushy shrubs up to 6 feet (1.8 m) in height and width, and are strong, hardy and easy to grow, in

The rugosa roses have attractive and healthy foliage, a long flowering season, and conspicuous hips. 'Frau Dagmar Hastrup' is one of the most compact, growing 4 to 5 feet (1.2 to 1.5m) high.

Rosa rugosa 'Frau Dagmar Hastrup'

country or in town. Many are genuinely perpetual flowering, and some single varieties have enormous hips, appearing while the plant is still in bloom. The leaves are fresh green and deeply veined (rugose means wrinkled) and turn yellow before they fade, contributing to the garden's autumn colour.

One of my favourites is 'Frau Dagmar Hastrup', with single pink flowers with yellow stamens all summer long, and huge, shiny, scarlet hips. For a hedge, nothing is more perfect than 'Sarah Van Fleet', which is more upright than most rugosas, growing to 6 feet (1.8 m), with soft, pink, semi-double flowers and as strong a scent as that of any rose I know. One caveat – it does not do well on chalk, where several rugosas tend to chlorosis.

For sheer depth of colour, there is 'Roseraie de l'Haÿ', with crimson double flowers, also highly scented, and for a white rose, there is the celebrated semi-double, scented 'Blanc Double de Coubert', which makes a very large bush indeed. I also have a weakness for a rugosa with quite a different look. 'Pink Grootendorst' has clusters of quite small frilled flowers like little carnations, but it is a martyr to greenfly.

Most rugosas should be planted 5 feet (1.5 m) apart, though for the narrower hedging varieties 4 feet (1.2 m) is enough. They do not need much pruning. They will put up with poor soil (except for the minority with a chalk problem), and a cold position. They look charming underplanted with the low ground cover of the purple-leaved *Viola labradorica*.

Rosa 'The New Dawn'

This is my favourite rambler, delightful in colour, scent and behaviour. A sport of the well-loved, shell-pink double rose 'Dr

The rambler roses generally flower only once but 'The New Dawn', a sport of a once-flowering rambler, repeats reliably after the mid-summer flush. This sweetly scented rose will grow to about 12 feet (3.6 m).

Sidalcea malviflora

Van Fleet', 'The New Dawn' resembles her parent in every way but one, where she surpasses him. Instead of flowering once only in a glorious burst, 'The New Dawn' flowers continuously after the first mid-summer flush well into the autumn. It is sweetly scented and has beautiful leaves, small, glossy, and blessedly free from mildew. It will grow to at least 12 feet (3.6 m) on a wall or tree, and is fully hardy. Another virtue is that when the flowers fade, the petals fall gently to the ground so that the plant is always fresh, whereas some ramblers, like 'Albertine', cling to their dead flowers and look brown and dusty when their brief season of glory is past.

'The New Dawn' makes a perfect companion for a clematis twining among the branches, and the old favourite, *C.* x *jackmanii* 'Superba', with velvety, dark purple sepals, makes exciting stabs of colour against the gentle pink of the rose.

Prune the rose tactfully in autumn, cutting out some of the older branches and tying in new shoots, and cut back the clematis in early spring. Give both plants a good mulch of compost or manure in winter, and make sure that the roots of the clematis are shaded in summer either by the rose itself, or with tiles or stones.

Sidalcea malviflora

The mallows are an attractive botanical family. Even the common wild mallow, flowering in dusty waste places in the heat of summer, is a welcome sight when wild flowers are scarce. In the garden, there are shrubby mallows, perennial mallows and annual mallows, all characteristic funnel-shaped flowers.

Sidalcea malviflora, a native of California, is a herbaceous perennial which likes full sun, though not drought conditions. It has satiny flowers in various shades of pink and shallow-lobed leaves, which form a ground-covering clump. One of several good garden varieties is the pure pink 'Rose Queen', which grows to 40 inches (1 m) tall, an excellent middle-of-the-border plant flowering for weeks from mid-summer. Keep it well away from the yellow daisy plants which rule the garden at this season, and plant it with

Sidalcea malviflora, a native of California, is a hardy herbaceous perennial of the mallow family. The garden varieties are clump-forming plants, growing to about 40 inches (100 cm).

Rosa 'The New Dawn'

blue thistle flowers (*Eryngium* or *Echinops*) or perhaps with white roses, especially 'Iceberg', a tall rose which can take a substantial ground cover. Rue, sage, thyme and other plants from the herb garden would make a discreet edging.

Plant 2 feet (60 cm) apart in groups according to your space.

Spiraea × arguta

Spring has reached its peak when this graceful deciduous shrub bursts into blossom, the branches so weighed down with tiny white flowers that they form a fountain. Plant tall Darwin tulips in front of the shrub and you have an unashamedly brilliant spring picture. When the flowers fade, small, fresh green leaves follow, which turn a gentle red in autumn, so *Spiraea* gives a long season of pleasure.

It is an easy shrub to grow in any well-drained soil, given a sunny position, making, rather slowly, a thicket 6 to 7 feet (1.8 to 2.1 m) tall. The one care it needs is careful pruning the moment the flowers have faded. Cut out old, weak shoots, especially from the centre of the bush,

Spiraea × arguta

and shorten the stems which have flowered, but *do not* cut away any of the new, leafy shoots which form very quickly, for it is these which will bear the flowers next year.

If you should decide to plant tulips with *Spiraea*, either take out the bulbs after flowering, and replace them with summer bedding plants, or leave the bulbs in and interplant with early perennials, such as hardy geraniums, which will hide their decaying stalks with young foliage.

Tulipa hybrids

In a general gardening book it is impossible to select a handful of tulips from the thousands available, and probably the gardener already has his favourites — perhaps charming little species for a rock garden, or handsome Darwins for a splash of spring bedding. Here I restrict myself to choosing two kinds of tulip of which I am particularly fond, lily-flowered tulips and parrot tulips.

Lily-flowered tulips have narrow, slender flowers with long pointed petals which reflex when open; being less ostentatious than Darwins, they blend better with other flowers in a mixed border, providing colour in late spring when the summer perennials are still in the foliage stage. My favourite variety is 'Captain Fryatt', a claret-coloured tulip 18 inches (45 cm) tall with slender but strong stalks which stand up well to the wind. A group of at least ten bulbs would go well near a group of the pure white 'White Triumphator', with the leaves of hardy geraniums or delphiniums pushing up between. There are other lily-flowered varieties in violet, pink, purple, gold and red. I leave mine in the border for two years, but after that they tend to decline.

My other choice — a vulgar one to many — is parrot tulips, because they recall the old fringed and stripy tulips in Dutch flower paintings. My parrots, it is true, are modern hybrids, with large fringed flowers which repel some connoisseurs, but I revel in them. 'Fantasy'

In late spring the arching branches of *Spiraea* × *arguta* are thickly clustered with small white flowers. This deciduous shrub, which grows to a height and spread of 7 feet (2.1 m), generally colours well in autumn.

Parrot tulips

There are tulips for the full three months of spring. 'Captain Fryatt', which grows to about 18 inches (45 cm), is a mid-season, lily-flowered variety with shapely blooms.

is a rose-pink tulip with a green stripe, flowering in late spring, and in some years I grow them in a formal row in a narrow bed under a wall with (we all have our clichés) forget-me-nots. A more brilliant variety is 'Orange Favourite', orange-scarlet feathered with green. Although it is claimed that the modern parrot tulips have strong enough stems to carry the flowers, I think they are safer planted out of the wind.

Follow the usual planting instructions for bulbs: well-drained soil and holes three times the depth of the bulbs. Plant tulips about 6 inches (15 cm) apart.

Viburnum carlesii
'Aurora'

This is an excellent shrub for the small garden, for it grows slowly into a compact, round shape not much more than 4 feet (1.2 m) high. It is deciduous, hardy

Viburnum carlesii

and happy in any soil, with two periods of interest in the course of the year, a long one in spring, and a shorter one in autumn, when the leaves turn red.

Its large, rounded clusters of tiny flowers open in late spring, but before that there are several weeks when the buds are a deep rosy pink of porcelain beauty. When they open, the flowers are first pale pink, then white, with a strong, sweet scent. The downy leaves are a broad oval shape, and are frankly rather dull. 'Aurora' makes a good specimen shrub in a small lawn, but you would need a later-flowering specimen shrub in another bed, perhaps a *Philadelphus*, to catch the eye in summer. It also looks

Viburnum carlesii is a compact deciduous shrub, rarely more than 4 feet (1.2 m) high. The waxy flowers, in some varieties red or deep pink in bud, are strongly scented. There is good leaf colour in autumn.

well in a sunny border with something blue, like forget-me-nots, at its feet.

Viburnum carlesii is a parent of a fine hybrid, *V. × burkwoodii*, which many prefer. It is taller, more open in structure, and evergreen, with bright green, glossy leaves which turn scarlet in autumn; it does well in towns. But *V. × burkwoodii* is brownish in the bud, and the rosy buds of 'Aurora' mean a lot to me. The answer is to find space for both.

Weigela florida
'Variegata'

This is to me the most beautiful weigela, although the tree and shrub guru, W.J. Bean, in a testy mood, wrote that it had 'a virus-ridden look'. I find the green-and-yellow leaves more spirited than the undistinguished plain green leaves of other varieties. However that may be, there are several weigelas which are excellent garden shrubs, hardy and reliable, easy to grow in any soil, and prodigal with their clusters of pink or red flowers in early summer. They grow about 6 feet (1.8 m) tall, and the branches arch over when heavy with blossom.

It is important to prune the shrub after flowering, shortening all spent shoots, after which new shoots will quickly form to carry flowers next year. These young shoots (sticking to my point, *pace* Bean) provide attractive variegated foliage for cutting in late summer, when good leaves may be scarce. Put them in a bowl with a handful of white or yellow daisies.

This weigela is so hardy that it makes a good shelter plant for smaller, slightly

Weigela florida 'Variegata' is a hardy deciduous shrub that will grow to a height of about 6 feet (1.8 m). In late spring and early summer pale pink flowers blend with the creamy variegation.

Weigela florida 'Variegata'

tender shrubs, such as daphne or *Osmanthus delavayi*, which has tiny, white, strongly scented flowers in spring. A close-planted mixed group of such as these on a shrub bank, protected by one weigela or more, could be underplanted with small spring bulbs.

Wisteria sinensis

This glorious giant of the garden has come to us through a charming act of Chinese generosity. In 1816 two small plants from the garden of a Chinese merchant in Canton, named Consequa, were presented to British friends who sent them home, and it is probable that nearly every wisteria grown in our gardens is descended from these two parents. Consequa was so well liked in the British community that when he died he earned an obituary in *The Times*.

Given its head, a wisteria will climb to 80 feet (15 m) or more and spread even further on each side of the stem. It is a confirmed climber, growing in an anti-clockwise direction, and will twist its way round pergolas, balustrades, tree trunks, or (be wary) drainpipes, even round its own stem. In late spring the plant becomes a waterfall of drooping racemes of mauve pea-flowers which blend exquisitely with the long pinnate leaves of fresh, bright green. There is often a smaller crop of flowers in late summer.

Wisteria needs sunshine and a good, but not excessively rich soil. It needs strong support and pruning twice a year – a hard pruning back to two or three buds on each shoot in winter, and a lighter summer pruning. In chilly countries it does best on a south wall or sheltered terrace, but in Italy is often grown up forest trees.

In view of its size and vigour, is it worth attempting a wisteria on a small house? Yes, certainly, if you are a handyman or handywoman who is not afraid of ladders (there is a splendid specimen on our village shop), but wisteria cannot be neglected, and must be properly trained from the start. It can even be pruned hard to make a small standard, but I consider this a brutality.

The familiar mauve species is perhaps the best against stone or mellow brick, but there is a lovely white form, 'Alba', for walls of newer, brighter brick, and also a double form, 'Plena'.

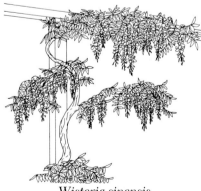

Wisteria sinensis

Wisteria sinensis is an exceptionally vigorous climber, capable of growing to 80 feet (15 m) or more. The mauve flowers, which hang in graceful racemes, are deliciously scented.

THE DRY
SUNNY GARDEN

Spiky leaves and spiny flowers, silvery foliage and felty stalks – many of the plants which thrive in dry soil are not sentimentally pretty, but please the eye with bold form or strange texture, especially those which flower in high summer and are armoured by nature to face the sun. This is one of the compensations for owners of a dry garden, with fast-draining sandy, gravelly or chalky soil.

Another is that many plants for the dry garden are deliciously aromatic, often natives of the Mediterranean, where so many herbs spring from the thin soil of the *maquis*. (If you approach the Greek island of Thasos by sea and the wind is right, you may smell the herbs half a mile away.) The dry garden is not the easiest to plant, but it brings unusual pleasures.

The plants which I have chosen for this chapter should prosper in a hot position, but this does not mean that they like to be starved, for they are not desert plants. With a few exceptions (which I have pointed out in each case), they like to be planted with plenty of decayed vegetable matter to hold the moisture, and mulched occasionally later on. Crumbly leaf-mould, compost or spent hops will counter the aridity.

Most of these plants will not need watering once they are properly established. One or two, such as *Campanula carpatica*, may sometimes flag in a drought, and you will have to water them, but the rest will find enough moisture to carry on, especially those, like *Acanthus*, which have very deep roots.

LEFT A raised bed marking a division in the garden makes an ideal home for plants such as pinks that like sun and sharp drainage.

ABOVE A dark ball of clipped box makes a simple accent in a bed of *Stachys olympica*, with grey foliage that is best in full sun.

These plants for the dry garden look best in association with each other, or with similar plants from the wide range of sun-lovers, including small-leaved shrubs, like bay and myrtle, which are characteristic of the Mediterranean. Some shade-lovers can be persuaded to grow in the sun, but they do not 'look right'. The dry garden has a harmony of its own.

Acanthus spinosus

Here there is a difficult choice between *Acanthus spinosus* and *A. mollis*, for both are fine architectural plants for the medium or large garden. *A. spinosus* is invincibly invasive and horribly spiny to handle, but is so spectacular in flower and leaf that I give it pride of place. A hardy perennial, flowering in late summer, it is celebrated for its enormous, deeply cut leaves of shiny dark green, said to have

Acanthus spinosus

been the inspiration in classical times of the Corinthian capital. (The leaves of *A. mollis* are rounded, and of a blander green.) The flower spikes, which are at least 4 feet (1.2 m) tall, carry hooded purple and white flowers up most of the

Varieties of *Achillea filipendulina* are reliable border perennials that flower in mid-summer. One of the tallest is 'Gold Plate', with flat heads of yellow flowers on stems 4 feet (1.2 m) tall.

stalk, and are plentiful if the plant is in full sun. In shade, it will be mainly a foliage plant, but still fully worth its place. It needs deep, well-drained soil.

Both species make a wonderful foil for shrub roses (again, not for the small garden), and they look well in the mixed border with sun-lovers such as achilleas and salvias, but their invasiveness is frankly a peril. If you can give them a bed to themselves, the leaves and flowers will make a strong focal point in the garden for weeks in late summer and autumn, and the flower spikes dry well for winter flower arrangements.

Achillea filipendulina 'Gold Plate'

The herbaceous flowers of high summer are apt to be sturdy to the point of coarseness, as they have to be able to

Acanthus spinosus is a handsome herbaceous perennial with deeply cut dark green leaves, which are very spiny. In summer stems about 4 feet (1.2 m) tall carry hooded flowers that are purple and white.

stand up to the sun – the gentle frailness of spring flowers is in the past. *Achillea*, or yarrow, is no exception, but it is a fine plant, nonetheless, with flat heads of tiny daisy flowers which stare boldly at the blue sky overhead. 'Gold Plate' is one of the taller varieties, with stalks 4 feet (1.2 m) high carrying very large, bright yellow flowers and, in my experience, needs no staking. The leaves are feathery and aromatic. 'Gold Plate' looks well in the company of the globe thistle, *Echinops*

Achillea 'Moonshine'

ritro, with steely blue globular flowers, as does the equally popular *A.* 'Moonshine', a shorter plant with lemon-yellow flowers and silvery leaves. (This variety flops a bit if not supported.)

'Gold Plate' should be planted in autumn in any well-drained soil in a sunny bed or border, in groups of three or five plants, 2 feet (60 cm) apart. It should be cut down in autumn and divided, if necessary, in spring. The flowers dry well for winter arrangements.

Allium species

Alliums are bulbs with a childish charm which best suits a cottage garden or an informal planting, though they also look well among shrub roses. They flower in round terminal umbels on stiff stalks but there are a great many species to choose from in a variety of colours and sizes. They are hardy and easy to grow and increase by clumping up and (in most cases) seeding freely.

Out of a large genus I suggest three alliums which are particularly delectable. The tallest is *A. giganteum*, with tight balls of violet flowers which in mid-summer top stalks that are 4 feet (1.2 m) tall. Equally handsome is *A. christophii* (also known as *A. albopilosum*), with enormous round heads of starry metallic-purple flowers about 8 inches (20 cm) in diameter on stalks 18 inches (45 cm) tall, a lovely plant with hybrid musk roses like 'Buff Beauty' and 'Cornelia'. A most curious and interesting species with a different flower shape is *A. bulgaricum* (sometimes listed as *A. siculum*), where the flowerheads are not tight globes but bunches of hanging bells. In the bud stage each bell is enclosed in a tight papery sheath, which bursts to release a pink-and-white striped nodding bell. This stage lasts for two or three weeks in early to mid-summer when the bells turn upwards to form a tight pointed cluster. The stalks are at least 3 feet (90 cm) tall and need some herbaceous underplanting.

Alliums will grow in any well-drained soil in a sunny spot. Plant at a depth of about three times the size of the bulb. They are often recommended for cutting, but I find the onion smell too strong for the house.

Of the ornamental onions, *Allium christophii* is one of the most striking, with large heads of starry flowers on stalks about 18 inches (25 cm) tall. Here it makes an unusual companion for bearded irises.

Anthemis cupaniana, an aromatic herbaceous perennial, bears a long succession of marguerite-like flowers on stems up to 12 inches (30 cm) high over spreading grey-green cushions of foliage.

Anthemis cupaniana

This charming daisy, large-flowered as a wild marguerite, though at most 12 inches (30 cm) tall, grows from a mat of soft grey-green leaves which are finely dissected and aromatic. As the plant is fast-spreading but not invasive – it is easily pulled up if it goes too far – it is my ideal

Anthemis cupaniana

of a ground-cover plant. A small piece planted in spring will spread over two or three square feet of soil in the course of the summer, or will hang down gracefully over the edge of a wall.

The daisies begin to flower in early summer and continue for many weeks, and there are intermittent flowers in

autumn and even winter, when they can be gratefully picked for the house.

Anthemis cupaniana, a native of Italy, needs full sun and thrives in a dry border. Graham Thomas, who has written so authoritatively on ground-cover, recommends using it in this way with bearded irises. Like many plants with grey or silver leaves, it looks drab in rain, and may be reduced in a bad winter, but, as with *Stachys olympica*, there are always small pieces left, and every root will grow. Indeed, the plant is the better for being cut back every year.

If you are growing it for the first time, unless you want instant results, put the plants in as much as 2 feet (60 cm) apart, and they will soon join up.

Artemisia ludoviciana

This fine foliage plant from North America has leaves so covered with down as to be almost white. Growing to 3 feet (90 cm) or a little more, it is a mass of willow-shaped aromatic leaves through the summer, with sprays of tiny grey-white flowers later in the season. It is frankly invasive and needs a bit of propping, but the rewards are the soft, soothing colour it provides against the

Artemisia ludoviciana is a hardy herbaceous species, sometimes more than 3 feet (90 cm) in height, producing a mass of silvery white leaves. In late summer the greyish flowers blend with the foliage.

Artemisia ludoviciana

bright flowers of the summer border, and the lavish quantity of stems you will get for cutting.

A well-liked variety is 'Silver Queen', a shorter plant, but even more floppy, and with different leaves, much dissected as against the entire leaves of the species. It runs freely underground, and in the mixed border must be firmly controlled. Yet another useful artemisia is the bushy, non-invasive *A. absinthium* 'Lambrook Silver', a plant selected by Mrs Margery Fish, but the dissected leaves are grey rather than silver-white.

Like most silver and grey plants, the artemisias look beautiful against pink – pink roses, mallows, phlox – or against dark red, if you prefer a stronger contrast. I have seen *A. ludoviciana* as an effective foreground to the deep purple gallica rose 'Tuscany'.

Plant artemisias 18 inches (45 cm) apart in dry well-drained soil in full sun, and cut them down when they begin to look bedraggled at the close of autumn.

Aubrieta deltoidea

It is curious how few connoisseur gardening writers have ever paid much attention to aubrietas, though William Robinson is an honourable exception. Perhaps they are so commonly grown that the snobs are bored with them. Or perhaps Reginald Farrer, disparaging the whole family of Cruciferae, did them an ill turn. Yet, a dry wall of yellow-grey stone in the Cotswold hills, in Gloucestershire, curtained with mauve aubrieta in spring, is an unforgettable sight. Often every cottage in the village contributes a flowery mass.

Aubrieta deltoidea is a native of high, rocky places in southern Europe, and was discovered by the botanist Tournefort in 1700; he took with him on his expedition the botanical artist Claude Aubriet, who drew it on the spot. Today, garden varieties, rather than the species, are usually grown, varying in colour from mauve to various shades of red and purple. The plant is evergreen, mat-forming, long-lived and disease-free, so it has much on its side.

A true rock plant, not much more than 4 inches (10 cm) high, though spreading up to 2 feet (60 cm) in width, it looks best against stone, perhaps on the top of a retaining wall, or beside steps, or even in cracks in paving, where Robinson suggested sowing seeds. It likes dry well-drained soil and should be clipped over after flowering to keep the plant as a tidy mound.

It looks well with most of the spring rock plants, like white *Iberis sempervirens*, and with the later-flowering species tulips, like *Tulipa greigii*, growing nearby.

Berberis thunbergii 'Rose Glow'

Some gardeners will not grow *Berberis* because of their aggressive thorns, but many of the berberis family make compact and beautiful shrubs which are well worth their space. I suggest growing them not in the mixed border, where you will have to work among them, risking damage to your hands and eyes, still less as a hedge, which may wound you as much as invading burglars and cats, but in a shrub bank, where you need not go near them except to admire.

Berberis thunbergii, a native of Japan, is a neat deciduous shrub from 3 to 5 feet (90 to 150 cm) high with light green leaves which take on a fiery autumn colour. It has red berries in late summer. 'Atropurpurea' has purple leaves which open early in the year and deepen in colour in autumn. But the most striking variety is 'Rose Glow', with variegated pink-and-purple leaves on all the young shoots. There are small yellow flowers in summer, nestling among the clusters of leaves.

Grown on a bank, 'Rose Glow' could be tucked among grey-leaved shrubs and

Berberis thunbergii, like many of the barberries, is a spiny deciduous shrub, which grows 3 to 5 feet (90 to 150 cm) tall. 'Rose Glow' is a purple-leaved form with unusual pink and white variegation.

sub-shrubs, like *Phlomis fruticosa* and the large, sprawly lavender, usually listed as 'Dutch'. For spring, there could be groups of white narcissi which, once planted, would look after themselves. For later months, foxgloves could be allowed to naturalize, and Japanese anemones (*A.* × *hybrida*) could ramp as they please without invading other plants, as they do in the herbaceous border.

Berberis likes full sun and reasonably good soil, so work in humus at planting time. It does not need pruning.

The dense mauve, red or purple patches of *Aubrieta deltoidea* make bold splashes in the spring garden. The mounded foliage of this evergreen rock plant rarely grows more than 4 inches (10 cm) high.

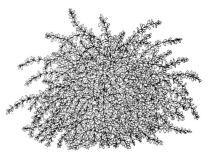

Berberis thunbergii 'Rose Glow'

Campanula carpatica

If you have a flowerbed bordered by a stone or brick path you will need cushiony plants to soften the hard edge of the path. *Campanula carpatica*, a native of the Carpathian Mountains in eastern Europe, is a perfect front-of-the-border plant which grows in low, rounded clumps which never straggle or encroach like some of the dwarf rock campanulas, which are almost weeds. It is also an excellent plant for the rock garden. It is herbaceous and hardy, grows up to 12 inches (30 cm) in height, and is covered for several weeks from mid-summer with fresh green, rounded leaves and wide-open bellflowers in blue, purple or white.

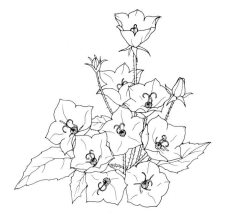

Campanula carpatica

In mid-summer *Campanula carpatica* produces many cup-shaped, blue flowers on stems up to 12 inches (30 cm) high. There are also white and purple forms of this herbaceous perennial.

There are a number of good named varieties in the catalogues and two or more colours can be grown side by side. The flowers look you in the face, rather than nodding, and are large for a plant of such modest size. The blue and purple forms contrast well with white pinks.

Plant them 12 inches (30 cm) apart in sun (though they will tolerate light shade) in well-drained garden soil.

Cheiranthus cheiri

Wallflowers have been a favourite cottage plant in Britain for centuries – Thomas Tusser, pundit on husbandry, recommended them in 1557 'for windows and pots'. They are still beloved for their velvety flowers in spring and for their rich scent. Bushy plants (if you have grown them well), they have upright sprays of usually single flowers in bronze, yellow, pink, orange and scarlet on woody stalks up to 2 feet (60 cm) tall. They need relatively mild winters to survive and are classic examples of plants best grown as biennials. They may be perennial in a good weather cycle.

The important thing in growing wallflowers is, after sowing seeds in early summer, to prick them out as soon as the seedlings are large enough, so that they can grow good roots before their final transplanting in autumn. That is why wallflowers are not a suitable plant for buying at garden centres, for they usually have too much top growth in proportion

Wallflowers, varieties of *Cheiranthus cheiri*, are best grown as biennials. The warm-scented, velvety flowers of 'Vulcan', an especially deep-coloured form, are borne on bushy plants up to 2 feet (60 cm) tall.

Cheiranthus cheiri

to their roots. When you finally plant them out, 16 inches (40 cm) apart, you must find a sheltered spot, for they hate wind, and they need dry, well-drained, limy soil. A narrow bed beneath a window is ideal.

Some gardeners sow them in a glorious mixture of colours. Others prefer to keep to one colour, in which case some tulips among them would lift the monotony, say pale yellow tulips with the scarlet wallflower 'Fire King', or purple tulips with the yellow 'Golden Monarch'. There is also a fine double yellow wallflower, dwarfer in size, called 'Harpur Crewe'.

Crocus speciosus

There is a handful of choice flowers which rejuvenate the autumn garden with a fresh look of spring, and *Crocus speciosus*, a native of the Near and Middle

Crocus speciosus

Crocus speciosus is an autumn-flowering species that naturalizes readily in grass but which is also suitable for growing in borders or among shrubs. The flowers, which stand 4 to 5 inches (10 to 12.5 cm) high, are in shades of lavender or mauve; there is also a fine white form.

East, is one of the most delightful. In early or mid-autumn it shoots up from the ground and opens within two or three days, often choosing its moment when there is rain after a long spell of drought. The flowers come before the long dark green leaves.

It is a bulb 4 to 5 inches (10 to 12.5 cm) high, with large, goblet-shaped flowers of variable colours, from pale lavender to deep mauve, or white in the variety 'Albus'. The petals have a delicate network of violet veins inside, and the conspicuous stamens have yellow anthers. It is a fine bulb for naturalizing, as

colonies build up quickly through clumping and seeding if the bulbs are left undisturbed.

Crocus speciosus is easy to grow in any well-drained soil and looks exciting in rough grass if you can time your mowing right, cutting the grass once or twice when the daffodils have died down, and holding back the final mowing until the crocus leaves have faded. It also looks well in a flower border among the Michaelmas daisies, but is perhaps best of all among shrubs, where the soft lilac and white will contrast happily with autumn colour. Plant the bulbs in late summer.

Dianthus hybrids

The first modern hybrid pink, with the merit of perpetual flowering, was bred in 1919, a cross between a perpetual carnation and an old white pink. For centuries before that, gardeners had adored pinks, many of which were exquisitely fringed or marked, and the 'florists', or growers who bred for competition, often artisans, especially in the north of Britain, developed hundreds of wonderful varieties – but they flowered once only.

Today, the modern pinks, sometimes listed as *D.* × *allwoodii*, are more widely grown, though they have by no means ousted the old-fashioned pinks, some of which have nostalgic names like 'Dad's Favourite'. The modern pinks usually flower for two months in mid-summer, and if regularly deadheaded, give a secondary show in autumn. The best make cushiony clumps of narrow grey evergreen leaves, and are heavily scented. A famous variety is 'Doris', with bright pink

Dianthus 'Betty Norden'

flowers with a salmon-pink ring in the centre on stalks 12 inches (30 cm) high. Many consider the colour too brash, but I know no pink which produces quite so many flowers. Another good variety is the dark crimson 'Ian'.

Of the old pinks, I love 'Dad's Favourite', a semi-double white pink with chocolate lacing, and 'Laced Romeo', creamy white with red lacing. And of course there is dear old double-flowered 'Mrs Sinkins', with all sorts of faults, such

as a short flowering season and a split calyx, but a thick border of 'Mrs Sinkins' sends a swooning scent far into the garden during its short and heady life.

Pinks need well-drained, preferably alkaline, soil, but it should not be ill-nourished or excessively dry. They should be planted about 12 inches (30 cm) apart in soil enriched with humus and bonemeal. Though hardy, pinks do not live for more than three or four years, but cuttings strike easily.

A good companion for pinks is *Festuca glauca*, a dwarf grass with tufts of blue-grey leaves.

Echinops ritro

The steel globe thistle, like the eryngiums (see page 59), has a spiky structure which often appeals to contemporary painters who view the garden in unsentimental terms. A tall plant, it has stout, branching stalks topped by round prickly heads of steely-blue flowers which give it its name, *echinos* being Greek for a sea-urchin or hedgehog. The large grey-green leaves are pinnate, and downy underneath, and have spiny tips. *Echinops ritro* flowers in

Echinops ritro

mid- to late summer, will grow in any soil, and needs no staking. It has great attraction for moths and bees.

I think the metallic blue looks best with yellow flowers, and suggest the rounded shrub *Hypericum* 'Hidcote' behind, which will be covered with large, yellow, saucer-shaped flowers in the same months, and, of the herbaceous yellow summer

The hybrid pinks, many spicily scented, have been bred from perennial species of *Dianthus*. Most grow from 10 to 16 inches (25 to 40 cm) tall, and the modern pinks are repeat-flowering.

The metallic blue, globular flowerheads of *Echinops ritro*, which can be cut for drying, appear from mid- to late summer. This tall herbaceous perennial grows to about 4 feet (1.2 m).

Eryngium × oliverianum

plants, the verbascums, or mulleins, would associate well.

Plant *E. ritro* in full sun in a group of three plants (for a bed of middling size) 2 feet (60 cm) apart. Certain varieties, of which 'Taplow Blue' and 'Veitch's Blue' are outstanding, have flowers of a more intense blue than the species.

Eryngium × oliverianum

This spiky herbaceous perennial is related to the sea holly which still grows wild on a few sandy shores in Britain. It is a striking plant for the summer border, both flowers and stalks being a metallic steely blue. The leaves are blue-green, spiny and deeply cut. It grows 2 to 3 feet (60 to 90 cm) tall, and the branching stalks bear glinting conical flowers circled with bristly bracts, like those of wild teasel. Miss Jekyll, skilful with words as well as plants, described it as having 'an admirable structure of a dry and nervous quality'.

It needs a dry, sunny place with very good drainage – sandy or chalky soils suit it well – and the roots go very deep, making it impervious to drought. The artist John Piper, 'a great man for thistles', grows it in the parallel borders of his farmhouse garden in the Chilterns, with echinops, giant annual sunflowers, rudbeckias, golden rod, and other traditional cottage flowers. It is excellent for cutting and drying for winter bouquets.

Three plants, 18 inches (45 cm) apart, would make an exciting group in any flower border, though Miss Jekyll, usually working on a grand scale, used eryngiums in bold masses.

Some gardeners prefer the taller *E. giganteum*, with paler, silvery flowers, known as 'Miss Willmott's Ghost', but this is biennial, and must be re-sown.

The eryngiums are striking herbaceous perennials well suited to dry summer borders. *Eryngium × oliverianum*, which is from 2 to 3 feet (60 to 90 cm) tall, has steely blue bracts surrounding the flowerheads.

Euphorbia characias wulfenii is an evergreen sub-shrub up to 4 feet (1.2 m) tall that is not fully hardy. It is worth growing, though, for its blue-green foliage and the dense, yellow flowerheads in early summer.

known as a sun-loving plant, it will also prosper in light shade. But it is sun-loving plants, like santolina and lavender, which make its most natural companions — it does not look right with anything lush. It needs reasonably good well-drained soil. Take cuttings every spring as an insurance against possible winter loss so that you have young plants in reserve. Some botanists class *E. characias* and *E. wulfenii* as separate species.

Euphorbia myrsinites

When I first saw this plant I thought it was a sedum, for the leaves are much fleshier than those of the other euphorbias I know, admittedly only a tiny fraction of this huge genus of some two thousand

The top of a low wall or a sunny spot in the rock garden are good places for *Euphorbia myrsinites*, a fleshy-leaved, evergreen species with trailing stems about 12 inches (30 cm) long but only 6 inches (15 cm) high.

Euphorbia characias wulfenii

Many gardeners have spectacular and well-established specimens of this beautiful sub-shrub to show with pride, but I confess that in our recent horrific winters I have not found it hardy. But it is so handsome that I persevere, and in sheltered gardens, there is less of a problem.

A bushy evergreen sub-shrub, *E. characias wulfenii* has stems which grow to 4 feet (1.2 m). They are covered at least half the way up with narrow glaucous leaves, and above that there will grow in early summer large cylindrical heads closely packed with saucer-shaped flowers, consisting of yellowish-green bracts with a pale orange eye. The stems can be very plentiful on a good plant.

Euphorbia characias wulfenii looks best as a specimen, not in groups, perhaps against a dry-stone wall, and though best

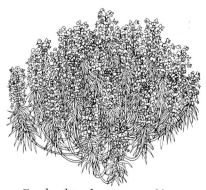

Euphorbia characias wulfenii

plants. It is a strange but effective little evergreen plant no more than 6 inches (15 cm) high, but with trailing stems a foot (30 cm) long growing all round the plant from the centre, packed with blue-grey fleshy leaves. The flowers at the tips of the stalks consist of sulphur-yellow bracts, and appear in spring.

This euphorbia needs well-drained soil, and looks best planted in groups of five plants or more placed 16 inches (40 cm) apart, to make a pool of glaucous colour in a sunny corner; or they can be planted

Euphorbia myrsinites

Many of the brooms, including *Genista lydia*, are very free-flowering. In early summer this shrub, when mature about 2 feet (60 cm) high and up to 5 feet (1.5 m) across, is a mass of yellow pea-flowers.

on top of a low wall, or against the south wall of a building. In this case, a low, flat climber on the wall behind would make an interesting background, such as a scarlet *Chaenomeles speciosa*, formerly known as 'japonica'.

Genista lydia

This cheerful shrub is ideal for a small, sheltered garden where winters are mild. A dwarf species from eastern Europe, it is smothered with yellow pea-flowers in early summer. Its nature is to tumble downhill, so plant it on a low wall or by steps and it will make a waterfall of colour for several weeks.

Genista lydia needs full sun and well-drained, even dry soil. Clip the tips of the grey-green shoots after flowering, but give it no serious pruning. It will grow in time to 2 feet (60 cm) in height, and 4 or 5 feet (1.2 to 1.5 m) in width, but not for several years, when it will have reached old age and may need replacing.

It is not an exciting plant when the flowers are over, so hardy annuals might be grown nearby to provide colour later in the season. Shirley poppies like the same conditions, and flower continuously through late summer and autumn in marvellous shades of red, pink and white. One of the pleasures of summer is to watch the crumpled buds bursting from their woolly coats, to smooth out within hours into handsome satiny flowers.

Genista lydia

Geranium 'Johnson's Blue'

This is, of course, a hardy geranium, not one of the half-hardy bedding pelargoniums, and is a long-flowering hybrid of the wild meadow cranesbill which is still plentiful in fields and by the wayside. It is a faultless border plant, forming cushions of deeply lobed leaves with an infinite number of flat mauve-blue flowers springing up from the clumps for at least two months from mid-summer. Few plants are so prolific and engaging while giving so little trouble. The flower stems

Geranium 'Johnson's Blue'

'Johnson's Blue', a hardy herbaceous geranium, bears blue flowers in profusion over a long season in summer. They float above mounds of deeply lobed leaves that stand about 16 inches (40 cm) high.

Helianthemum nummularium, the rock rose, has many short-lived flowers in quick succession. This shrubby evergreen grows to 12 inches (30 cm), spreading to 2 feet (60 cm).

are about 16 inches (40 cm) tall.

Plant 16 inches (40 cm) apart in ordinary garden soil, and divide the clumps every few years. This geranium can be grown as a front-of-border plant, associating with almost any summer plant you can think of — alchemilla, grasses, other varieties of geranium, perhaps lilies. Or use it in groups as ground-cover for a rosebed. There is a white form of the meadow cranesbill which is just as attractive as the blue.

I am also fond of another blue geranium which is a parent of 'Johnson's Blue', *G. himalayense*, usually listed as *G. grandiflorum*, a larger plant than its offspring,

on the ground. Next morning, the plant will be covered with fresh flowers.

They want full sun and well-drained soil, and should be clipped over after flowering like *Iberis*. They are not usually long-lived and it is wise to take cuttings of favourite varieties in summer to keep up your stock. 'Ben Afflick' is a good copper variety, and 'Wisley Primrose' a good yellow. There are also double varieties but I do not like them, for the simple beauty of the flower is quite lost.

Plant helianthemums 2 feet (60 cm) apart, perhaps with one colour overlapping another, such as bronze with yellow, or pink with white.

Helianthemum nummularium

Hypericum × inodorum 'Elstead'

The shrubby hypericums flower at a welcome time in the height of summer, when the early summer blossom is finished and the hydrangeas are still to come. They put on a glorious show of golden flowers over weeks, and are a feature of the Cottage Garden at Sissinghurst, where Harold Nicolson, husband of Vita Sackville-West, had his own plot and indulged his taste for scarlet, yellow and 'sunset' flowers at every season. He grew it near golden privet, orange potentillas, scarlet dahlias and red hot pokers.

'Elstead' is one of the most valuable hypericums, having the double interest of berries as well as flowers. Making a mound 4 feet (1.2 m) tall and as much or more in width, it bears cup-shaped flowers in profusion, and scarlet oval berries at the same time, which is most

Hypericum 'Hidcote'

unusual. It is hardy, is a good town plant, and is said to be 'semi-evergreen', a flattering description, for there are few leaves left in a hard winter.

In very cold gardens, *H.* 'Hidcote' is a better choice, being more reliably hardy. It is a taller shrub, and the golden flowers are larger and finer, but there are no berries.

Both shrubs like full sun, are easy as to soil, and should be clipped over in spring.

Hypericum × *inodorum* 'Elstead' is a semi-evergreen shrub that grows to a height of 4 feet (1.2 m). The yellow, cup-shaped flowers are borne freely and followed by showy berries.

with deeper blue flowers. But its flowering period is short and it needs a bit of propping, so if you have to choose, 'Johnson's Blue' has more to give.

Helianthemum nummularium

Helianthemums, or rock roses, are among the most charming of plants for spilling over steps or low walls. Rather shrubby in texture, and evergreen, they grow at most 12 inches (30 cm) high, but spread sideways to at least 2 feet (60 cm), producing a profusion of small, rose-like flowers from early summer. These come in a range of red, orange, bronze, yellow, pink and white, and are well stocked by nurseries and garden centres. One of the charms of rock roses when in flower is that they bloom in the morning and then shed their petals to make a ring of colour

In spring the evergreen leaves of the shrubby candytuft, *Iberis sempervirens*, are smothered by white flowers. Low mounds, about 9 inches (23 cm) high, are up to 3 feet (90 cm) across.

Iberis sempervirens

No plant in the garden has flowers of a purer white than the shrubby candytuft, which makes a low, rounded cushion so compact that it is ideal for a small garden in country or town. It is evergreen, and in spring the leafy cushion is smothered with a snowy blanket of four-petalled flowers which last for several weeks. In time it will spread to as much as 3 feet (90 cm).

Iberis sempervirens needs a sunny spot, and well-drained soil, preferably limy, is essential. A natural position would be at the top of a low wall; if grown in a garden with heavy soil, like London clay, the bed should be raised a foot or so and grit worked in to improve the drainage, an effort which is well worth while as it will also benefit the surrounding plants. Given sun and drainage, this iberis is totally reliable and rewarding. I like to clip mine over after flowering – the bare stems are soon clothed again with fresh young shoots.

This is a case where the obvious choice of companion plants is probably the best. Aubrieta and helianthemum enjoy the same conditions, and will tumble over the

wall making cascades of colour against the white of the candytuft. The best variety of this is called 'Snowflake'.

Lavandula 'Hidcote'

Lavandula 'Hidcote' is a favourite and easily recognizable lavender, for it is the variety with the darkest flowers, a deep purple. It is one of the best for a small garden, making a compact, shrubby plant 18 inches (45 cm) high, ideal for a low, neat hedge. It is not, however, the most highly scented. For scent, *L. spica*, or *L. angustifolia*, the 'old English lavender', is better, a larger, sprawlier plant with fewer flowers, but these of true lavender

The lavenders are evergreen shrubby plants, some of rather sprawling habit, but *Lavandula* 'Hidcote' makes a neat, upright bush about 18 inches (45 cm) high and the flowers are a v̄ery dark purple.

blue, and with very narrow grey leaves. It is the lavender traditionally used for drying, for which purpose the flowers should be picked in the bud.

Plant dwarf lavenders 12 inches (30 cm) apart in the sun in well-drained soil, the taller kinds 18 inches (45 cm) apart. Deadhead in autumn after flowering, and

clip the plants hard in early spring. If not used for hedges, lavenders make attractive groups in a border, or a short row of from four to six plants could be planted under each front window of your house. Lavenders are not long-lived, but cuttings

Lavandula 'Hidcote'

taken in summer strike easily in a frame, or even in the open ground, so that you will have young plants to replace the old ones when, after four or five years, they have grown woody and brittle.

Nerine bowdenii

The standard instructions for growing this bulb are not always correct, and I have revised my old-fashioned views after consulting a celebrated nerine grower who has collected and observed many nerines in the wild. In their native home, South Africa, they do not grow in clumps, but the large flowers shoot up from single, scattered bulbs.

The only species hardy in Britain is *N. bowdenii*, which is leafless and dormant in winter, and can therefore take cold weather, though other species can be grown under glass. The exotic-looking flowers grow in large, well-rounded umbels of up to eight bluish-pink flowers on bare stalks, and bloom in autumn, when there is little of this colour in the garden. Contrary to received wisdom, the bulbs should be planted in late summer as much as 6 to 8 inches (15 to 20 cm) deep, and 5 inches (12.5 cm)

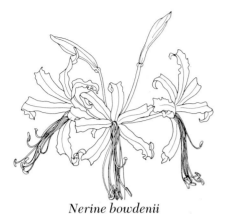

Nerine bowdenii

The Jerusalem sage, *Phlomis fruticosa*, revels in a hot dry position. This evergreen sub-shrub makes a sprawling bush of grey-green leaves about 4 feet (1.2 m) high. Flowering starts in mid-summer.

'Fenwick's Variety', with larger and deeper pink flowers than the species. There are other species and varieties in various shades of red, pink, orange and white, but they are not hardy. I personally think that nerines look best on their own, perhaps in a narrow bed under a wall. The flowers are wonderful for cutting.

Phlomis fruticosa

Phlomis fruticosa, or Jerusalem sage, is an evergreen sub-shrub native to hot, dry countries in the Middle East and to some of the Mediterranean islands, including Malta and Sicily, so it will take any amount of baking. Growing to 4 feet (1.2 m) in height and perhaps 2 feet (60 cm) in width, the stems are massed with pairs of grey-green hairy leaves, and the plant has a somewhat dusty look until mid-summer, when its arresting flowers bring it to life. These grow in whorls on the stalks, and are hooded, labiate and bright yellow. They flower in succession for about two months.

Phlomis fruticosa should prove hardy on a dry, sunny bank and looks best with

apart, in the poorest possible soil; if they form clumps, and the bulbs are forced to the surface, it means that the soil is too rich. Sand may be placed under the bulbs at planting time. In South Africa, nerines grow in light shade in the wild, but in cooler climates they need some sun and light, and, if possible, the protection of a wall. They are lime-tolerant, and should not be disturbed unless crowded clumps have formed despite your careful treatment.

The best form of *N. bowdenii* is

plants of similar origin, such as verbascums, rock roses, lavender and thyme. Alternatively, it will do well against the south wall of a house, where *Cotoneaster horizontalis* could be planted behind to give a dark green background to the grey-leaved shrub. This cotoneaster, grown as a climber, will go to 9 feet (2.7 m), moulding itself neatly to the wall and needing no support.

Nerine bowdenii. A South African bulb bears its pink flowers on stems up to 2 feet (60 cm) high in autumn, after the leaves have appeared. 'Fenwick's Variety' is the most vigorous form.

Phlomis fruticosa

are crinkly, of typical sage green.

This is not a plant for a singleton position. You want a group of at least three plants in a border, perhaps with yellow summer perennials behind, such as *Achillea* 'Moonshine', a pale yellow yarrow of medium height with silvery leaves, or the taller *A. filipendulina* 'Gold Plate', with large, flat heads of bright yellow, or the best of the verbascums, 'Gainsborough'. For yet more contrast, you could add to the group the scarlet campion, *Lychnis chalcedonica* – and why be shy of a strong colour scheme in the mid-summer sun?

Salvia × *superba* needs regular dead-heading, even a seemingly callous shearing to the ground while there are still a

Lavender cotton, *Santolina chamaecyparissus*, is a shrubby evergreen that can be used as a low hedging plant 12 to 18 inches (30 to 45 cm) high. It has button-like flowers.

There are good ornamentals as well as herbs in the sage family. *Salvia* × *superba* is a hardy herbaceous perennial that will grow to 3 feet (90 cm). Flowering lasts through the second half of summer.

Salvia × superba

This plant is not, perhaps, a star in its own right, but is a great feature player, a foil for other more brilliant plants. It is a hardy perennial of the invaluable sage family, happy in any soil so long as the position is sunny, flowering from mid-summer for many weeks. The plant is bushy, branching into many spikes of blue flowers enclosed by crimson bracts, the colours combining into intense purple when the flowers are fresh. The bush grows to a height of some 3 feet (90 cm) and 18 inches (45 cm) across. The leaves

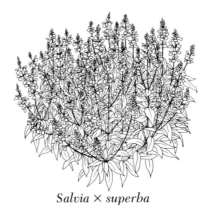

Salvia × *superba*

few buds unopened. You will be rewarded by a fresh new crop of flowers in early autumn.

Santolina chamaecyparissus

This atttractive little evergreen sub-shrub from the Mediterranean, also called lavender cotton, has been grown in Britain since the sixteenth century, both as a medicinal herb, as a drying plant, and as a clipping plant to edge parterres and knot gardens. It rivals lavender as a neat plant for a low garden hedge.

The small bushes, 12 to 18 inches (30 to 45 cm) high, are so covered with a woolly protective felting that they are almost white. The whole plant is crowded with small, narrow, feathery leaves which are aromatic, the smell being rather pungent, and in late summer long-stalked heads of small yellow flowers appear, like tiny balls of wool. The colour is coarse, and, as with other

Santolina chamaecyparissus

silver-leaved composite plants, like *Senecio*, the plant is prettier without them.

Today, lavender cotton is usually grown in the herb garden, where it looks appropriately trim and tidy. Sometimes it is used as an edging to formal rosebeds, but the yellow flowers are a distraction and some gardeners cut them off. It is also a good plant to put in groups at the front of a mixed border, providing attractive foliage to hide the stalks of very tall summer plants like achilleas.

Treat this santolina like lavender, putting in the plants 18 inches (45 cm) apart in sun in light, well-drained soil, and clipping them hard in spring. Take cuttings in late summer in case the plants succumb to a severe winter.

Scabiosa caucasica

The wild field scabious is a weed in my garden, but I like it enough to grow varieties of its grander relative, *S. caucasica*, an attractive hardy perennial for the late summer border, with rosettes of mauve flowers with yellow centres. Scabious is just the right plant to cool down the hot yellow daisy flowers which dominate the garden at this season. It is a splendid cutting plant, the long bare stems being about 2 feet (60 cm) long, and there are various shades of blue and purple available, as well as the excellent 'Bressingham White'. Scabious must have sun and very well-drained soil, and do not succeed on clay.

'Clive Greaves' is a good colour form of *Scabiosa caucasica*, a hardy perennial that flowers from mid-summer. Scabious are excellent for cutting and have flower stems up to 2 feet (60 cm) tall.

Sweet scabious, *S. atropurpurea*, is also a worthwhile plant, a hardy annual to fill gaps in late summer where delphiniums, lilies and other earlier flowers have died down. Do not despise an old-fashioned mixed packet of seeds, to be sown *in situ* in late spring, which will give you a surprise assortment of purple, red and white flowers up to 3 feet (90 cm) tall. There are also mixed packets of a dwarf form, 18 inches (45 cm) tall, in the same vivid colour range.

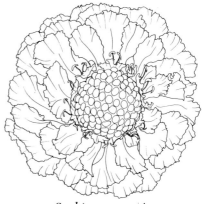

Scabiosa caucasica

Sedum 'Autumn Joy'

This splendid member of the huge stonecrop family, a herbaceous perennial, can claim to be interesting for three hundred and sixty-five days a year, the whole plant forming a neat, circular mound with changing assets.

In spring, the mound is low, and consists of rosettes of fleshy, waxy, pale green leaves. Throughout the summer, the mound grows in height to about 12 inches (30 cm), making a lovely foliage plant to fill in between summer perennials in the border. Then the flowering stalks appear, with toothed leaves all the way up, and each stalk is topped with a large flat head of pale green buds; this is perhaps the plant's most beautiful moment. By late summer, the buds have opened into clusters of small, deep coral-pink, starry flowers, and the stalks are 2 feet (60 cm) high. In autumn the flowers turn bronze, and finally brown. You can leave them on until late winter, and when you cut them, the new leaves will already be there.

In its bronze-pink prime, 'Autumn Joy' looks fine with other autumnal colours, and perhaps some yellow for lightness, and some silver in front. I have seen it planted alongside the shrubby *Potentilla* 'Elizabeth', with butter-yellow flowers still going strong, against a background of the shrub *Viburnum × burkwoodii*, which

Sedum 'Autumn Joy'

turns scarlet in autumn. In front of the bed was a silvery patch of *Stachys lanata*.

Plant 'Autumn Joy' in groups 18 inches (45 cm) apart in well-drained soil, not rich or heavy, and divide every three years or so in spring, for if the plant grows too large, the flowers tend to topple over.

Stachys olympica

One of this plant's country names is lamb's tongue, but another name, rabbit's ears, describes the soft, strokable quality of its leaves more aptly. Primarily a foliage plant, the thick silver leaves of *S. olympica* make a thick, fast-growing, evergreen ground-cover, the stems rooting wherever they touch the soil. After midsummer, woolly spikes about 18 inches (45 cm) tall, carrying tiny purple flowers all the way up, rise from the mat of foliage. The plant is hardy, needs full sun (like most silver plants), and prefers light soil; a sticky soil does not suit it.

This is one of the most popular of all ground-cover plants, going particularly well with old roses or peonies in a border, or with purple-leaved shrubs; it is also useful as foliage in an all-white garden, or, more prosaically, as a cover for awkward banks. It suffers in heavy rain, when, said Mrs Margery Fish, 'it looks like drowned rats'. It may also take a knock in a hard winter, but there are always enough scraps left to collect and replant in spring. There is a non-flowering variety called 'Silver Carpet', but it is liable to mildew.

Sedum 'Autumn Joy' is a herbaceous perennial with fleshy leaves that carries dense heads of starry flowers in late summer and autumn on stems up to 2 feet (60 cm) high.

The woolly leaves of *Stachys olympica* make a dense silvery mat. The flower spikes, up to 18 inches (45 cm) tall, are less important than the ground-covering foliage, which goes well with many plants, including old roses.

I suggest planting *S. olympica* sparsely to begin with, for economy's sake, and letting it run about until it fills your spaces, when you can pull up the surplus.

'*Verbascum* × *hybridum*

Some of the most majestic mulleins are the Cotswold hybrids, tall, striking plants with branching spires crowded with saucer-shaped flowers in late summer in yellow, pink, white, mauve or apricot. 'Gainsborough' is my favourite of the range because of its colour, which is a soft, pale, moonlight yellow. Grown in groups in a border it blends well with the deep blue of *Anchusa* or the steely blue of *Echinops;* there is a yellow and blue border at Clare College, Cambridge, where 'Gainsborough' mingles with del-phiniums, *Thalictrum*, and achilleas to make a perpendicular planting as Gothic as King's College Chapel in the back-ground. At the opposite end of the scale, a single plant can make an eye-stopping punctuation mark in a sunny wild garden, perhaps rising from a sea of *Lamium* or other ground-cover. Growing to 4 feet (1.2 m) from its basic rosette of large grey leaves, it must be given a stake.

Verbascums need full sun and well-drained soil but not, I think, very poor soil. A seed of wild common mullein once landed in my manure heap, and an enor-mous plant grew like Jack's beanstalk to a height of 5 feet (1.5 m).

'Gainsborough' is sometimes listed as a perennial, but is best treated as a biennial, for it is not long-lived. If grown in a group, plant 3 feet (90 cm) apart. Of the similar hybrids in other colours, 'Pink Domino', a pleasant rose-pink, is the best known.

Verbascum 'Gainsborough'

The mulleins are tall bold plants for the sunny border. One of the loveliest of the perennial hybrids is *Verbascum* 'Gainsborough', with branching spikes of pale yellow flowers up to 4 feet (1.2 m) tall.

THE MOIST
SUNNY GARDEN

The cheapness and ease with which garden pools can be made today have opened a new world to the gardener without a natural pond or stream. He can grow many moisture-loving plants in the boggy area that can be created beside a pool, and true aquatics in the pool itself. There are nurseries to supply the plants, and some excellent books telling him how to make and plant a pool, which must be in the sun and clear from overhanging trees.

Many of the best plants which thrive in moist, sunny places are species, and quite a number of them are natives of Britain. Long years ago, before the wild flowers grew scarce, the streamside was patterned with forget-me-nots, marsh mari-golds, globe flowers, irises, arrowhead, loosestrife, and other lush plants, many at their best after mid-summer. Even today, with all the varieties and the exotic species that are available to us, the waterside grows in beauty as the summer advances. Many of the plants have large, even enormous, leaves, and if the giants are too big for you, there is the superb but not overpowering foliage of rodgersia and rheum, and the cool, delicate leaves of some of the moisture-loving shrubs.

Some of the plants in this chapter will grow in moist soil without the presence of water, but most look more natural by the waterside, with reflections and ripples to enhance their charm.

LEFT There are many lush moisture-loving plants that look their best planted in an open position beside still or running water.

ABOVE Of bedding plants that thrive in rich moist soil dahlias are among the most varied in colour and form, giving a fine late-summer display.

Astrantia major

I have two favourite astrantias, *A. major* and *A. maxima*, and scarcely know which to put in first place. They are hardy perennials of the enchanting family Umbelliferae. They will grow in sun or light shade, but need a little permanent moisture, so if they are grown in sun, it should be in a cool, damp border.

Astrantia major, or masterwort, has been grown in Britain for centuries, a wholly delightful plant with deeply dissected leaves like those of hellebores, and branching stems of small posy flowers in white and green with a hint of pink. The posy consists of tiny green-and-white, pink-stalked flowers encircled by green bracts. The stems are 2 feet (60 cm) high and the plant blooms for many weeks from mid-summer, sometimes almost into winter. It seeds freely. There are various forms of the species of which I like best the form with variegated leaves, 'Sunningdale Variegated'.

Astrantia maxima is a less vigorous plant, but more conspicuous because the posies are a vivid rose-pink with pink bracts which are acid green on the reverse, making a highly sophisticated

Astrantia major

combination of colours. It comes from damp meadows in the Caucasus, and needs more moisture than *A. major*.

Astrantias are plants for close observation, so do not let them get swamped by coarse or garish perennials. They look well with phlox, which like the same conditions, but there is a case for putting the undemanding *A. major* in large groups, planted 18 inches (45 cm) apart, among shrubs like *Philadelphus* which are somewhat bare at the base and offer space for a choice underplanting. As the shrub will take its full share of moisture, the astrantias may need mulching.

The masterworts are herbaceous perennials of quiet beauty. The flowers of *Astrantia major*, born on stems up to 2 feet (60 cm) high, are a subtle blend of white, green and pink.

Cornus alba 'Elegantissima'

This dogwood gives joy all the year round. A fast-growing deciduous shrub which forms a thicket, it is a mass of

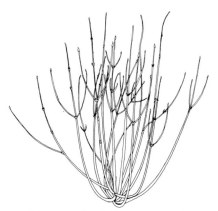

Cornus alba 'Elegantissima'

The variegated foliage of *Cornus alba* 'Elegantissima' is the chief asset of this dogwood in summer. Stooling produces young stems that are brilliant scarlet right through the winter months.

beautiful variegated leaves in spring and summer, pale green margined with creamy-white, which turn pinkish-gold in autumn before they fall. Then, all the young shoots on the bush are revealed as brilliant scarlet, and remain so through the winter. If you want the whole shrub to be a phalanx of scarlet stems, you must pollard it in early spring, cutting it to 8 inches (20 cm) from the ground, but if you do this you will have to wait some weeks for the new stems and leaves. (The flowers are small, white and not very interesting and, if you do not pollard, appear in early summer.) It is sometimes listed as *C. a.* 'Variegata'.

This shrub looks wonderful by water, especially in winter, but alternatively plant it against the dark background of cypress or yew. It is rather rampant, and the variety 'Sibirica', or Westonbirt dogwood, is neater for the small garden. Its stems are even more brilliant in winter, but the leaves are plain green, a considerable loss. Both varieties like moisture, but if watered well when young will establish in any good garden soil, including chalk.

Plant them in sun or light shade, either as single plants, or, if you want a large group, I suggest three plants 4 feet (1.2 m) apart.

Another excellent variety is 'Spaethii', with leaves variegated in green and gold.

Cornus kousa chinensis

Dogwoods are most commonly grown for their coloured winter stems, but this Chinese species has beautiful and curious flowers perched on short stalks which smother the bush in early summer like a cloud of cabbage white butterflies. The flowers consist of small, dark centres (the true flowers) like boot-buttons, surrounded by four large, lime-green bracts. As summer goes by, the bracts turn from green to white, and then to cream before they fade. The leaves turn red and bronze in autumn, and the fruits are like small strawberries, so that the season of interest is long. The shrub grows in horizontal tiers up to at least 15 feet (4.5 m) high and as much in spread. It is deciduous. Owing to its fine structure

Cornus kousa chinensis

it looks splendid planted near a building.

Though officially hardy, this is not a shrub for every garden. It needs moist acid or neutral soil and shelter from cold winds, and flowers most prodigally in full sun. Even so, it will take a few years to reach perfection. Gardeners with a cold garden or with alkaline soil would do better to choose one of the more adaptable members of the distinguished *Cornus* family – perhaps *C. alba* 'Sibirica'. If possible, plant this by a pool, where the red stems will be reflected in the water.

Cornus kousa chinensis is a dogwood that can grow to 15 feet (4.5 m) or more. In early summer, the flower bracts, first greenish white, then cream, smother the tiered growth.

The flower form and colour of the hybrid dahlias is very varied. 'Bishop of Llandaff', a cultivar that grows to 3 feet (90 cm), is one of the peony-flowered varieties of these half-hardy perennials. There are shorter dahlias but also others that are among the tallest-growing of bedding plants.

Dahlia hybrids

Dahlias, like delphiniums, are plants which you must choose for yourself, preferably in proud bloom at a flower show. There are many hundreds of varieties, and one which is ubiquitous one year may not be available the next, so I dare not recommend them, but I will discuss the pros and cons of growing them.

In favour is the fact that you like them, or, indeed, adore them, as do many gardeners who grow almost no other flowers, tending them like pedigree pets. Secondly, they are amongst the finest flowers for cutting, not if you are making a tasteful foliage arrangement for the dining-table, but if you want something showy to decorate the parish church.

Against growing dahlias is that you may not like them, finding them gaudy (I enjoy their flamboyance myself), and the hard fact that they are tremendously troublesome to grow – not difficult, but time-consuming.

Dahlias are tuberous plants which come to us from Mexico, and were named after a Swedish botanist, Andreas Dahl, who worked on them in Madrid in the eighteenth century. They are divided officially into a number of groups, Single-Flowered, Collerette, Water-lily, Pompon, Cactus and others, but for practical purposes there are two kinds, small dahlias up to 2 feet (60 cm) in height for bedding, usually grown as annuals from seed, and taller dahlias, up to 5 feet (1.5 m), for borders, which are perennial, but not hardy. Some gardeners grow these in the mixed border, where they are splendid for taking over in late summer after the early perennials, but others prefer to grow them in beds dedicated to dahlias only. The flowers can be enormous, up to 12 inches (30 cm) across.

Dahlias come in every conceivable colour except true blue. A few have dark foliage, instead of the usual bright green, and when I asked four first-rate gardeners, not specialists, to name their favourite dahlia, three chose 'Bishop of Llandaff', a blood-red peony-flowered variety 3 feet (90 cm) high, notable for its purple foliage.

The cultivation of dahlias is a year-round affair. They like full sun, good drainage, masses of food and a great deal of water. To skate briefly over the growing programme, the work starts in autumn, when you must dig the beds and work in rotted manure. In spring, work over the beds and sprinkle in some balanced fertilizer. Plant the tubers in late spring or early summer, according to your climate, giving each plant a stake, from 12 to 36 inches (30 to 90 cm) apart, depending on size. From then on, watch the plants, mulch, water and disbud, spray for greenfly, trap slugs and snails, and catch earwigs as best you can. (Canes topped by inverted flowerpots set as traps for earwigs are not a beautiful sight as you take a stroll round the garden in the twilight.) Enjoy the flowers from late summer until the first frost, when you lift the tubers and store them for next year. Dahlias are a madman's obsession, but gardening would not be the fun it is without our fanatics.

Doronicum 'Miss Mason'

In summer there are almost too many yellow daisy plants in the garden, but they are very welcome in spring, when they are scarce. One of the easiest to grow is *Doronicum*, an old herbaceous garden plant which forms a clump of heart-shaped leaves in early spring, with masses of cheerful bright yellow flowers on stems 18 inches (45 cm) tall; the leaves are shiny and have scalloped edges. 'Miss Mason' is one of the best of several good forms. The plant likes moisture, but not in great quantity, and a cool border with

Dahlia, cactus-flowered hybrid

any good garden soil in sun or light shade is the ideal situation. The clumps grow slowly and should not need dividing for several years. The plants should be put in 12 inches (30 cm) apart, with some peat to preserve moisture.

Doronicum is hardy and reliable and always generous with flowers; plant groups interspersed with white tulips, with blue flowers also in the picture. The tiny forget-me-not blossoms of *Brunnera macrophylla* would overlap with the *Doronicum*, and the foliage of peonies behind would make a dark background, with their flowers to follow.

The daisy flowers of *Doronicum* 'Miss Mason' brighten the spring garden. This hybrid grows to 18 inches (45 cm), the flowers standing above a good clump of bright green leaves.

Eupatorium purpureum is a tall herbaceous perennial, up to 8 feet (2.4 m) high, that will thrive with other lush plants at the water's edge. Care is needed when planting for it can be invasive.

Eupatorium purpureum

This North American species of hemp agrimony is taller and grander than the British native, *E. cannabinum*, rising to 8 feet (2.4 m) in height, with whorls of narrow leaves all the way up the purple stems, which are topped with huge sprays of purplish-pink flowers in late summer and early autumn. William Robinson called it 'a fine plant for the rougher parts of a garden', and it is best by the waterside; it can be seen in full splendour by the moat at Scotney Castle, in Kent, with meadowsweet and rushes, and water-lilies in the water. It can also be grown at the back of a moist border, where it may need a mulch of peat, but it is invasive and would need firm control.

Plant *E. purpureum* 3 feet (90 cm) apart in rich soil, preferably without lime.

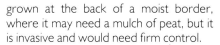

Eupatorium purpureum

Euphorbia griffithii

This is one of the best hardy perennials for any garden, large or small, making its mark in a border or corner bed in early summer. A plant from the Himalayas, it produces red stems up to 30 inches (75 cm) tall, lavishly dressed in narrow, olive-green leaves veined with red. The flowers at the top consist of round clusters of flame-coloured bracts. The finest variety is 'Fireglow', which I think looks best in a strong, hot colour scheme, perhaps with the shorter, bushier *Euphorbia polychroma*, with sulphur-yellow flowers, perhaps with yellow azaleas. Later,

'Fireglow', the form of *Euphorbia griffithii* most widely grown, lives up to its name in early summer, when the flower bracts are brick red over olive-green foliage. The clumps are up to 30 inches (75 cm) high.

Filipendula palmata

Anyone who has spotted our native meadowsweet (perhaps from a punt on a hot summer's day) revelling in the boggy land beside a stream will appreciate this larger and finer species from Siberia and Japan.

Filipendula palmata is a hardy herbaceous perennial with flower stems rising to 4 feet (1.2 m) from clumps of handsome dark green, five-lobed leaves. These stems are topped in mid-summer with flat, feathery heads of tiny pink flowers which fade to white. It needs rich, moist soil, with or without lime, and

Filipendula purpurea

Filipendula palmata is a herbaceous perennial suitable for waterside planting. The feathery pink flowerheads are carried on stems up to 4 feet (1.2 m) tall in mid-summer.

the leaves give good autumn colour.

Grow 'Fireglow' in any good garden soil, with or without lime, so long as it is reasonably moist. It will grow in shade but, if the shade is deep, the bracts are too green and lose their glow. Put in the plants 2 feet (60 cm) apart.

Euphorbia griffithii 'Fireglow'

associates well with water-loving irises, such as *I. laevigata*, or, if there is space, with trees and shrubs of the waterside, such as dogwoods and willows. A similar plant, with flowers of a deep cherry pink on crimson stems, is *F. purpurea*, which also has a white-flowered form, 'Alba'.

Plant 2 feet (60 cm) apart beside a stream, a natural pond, or a garden pool with water overlapping the margins.

Although too coarse for the border, the cartwheel flower, *Heracleum mantegazzianum*, is a bold and handsome umbellifer for the wild garden. The flower stem can reach a height of 12 feet (3.6 m).

Heracleum mantegazzianum

One of my favourite garden plants (yes, *garden* plants) is cow parsley. Think of this magnified to three or four times its size, and you have the spectacular *Heracleum mantegazzianum*, or cartwheel flower, a giant up to 12 feet (3.6 m) tall with rough, dissected leaves 3 feet (90 cm) wide at the base, and branching stems bearing huge white umbelliferous flowers in mid-summer. The plant is a biennial, but seeds all too freely, and it is as well to cut off most of the flowers before the seeds fall.

(It is best to wear gloves when handling the stems, as a few people are allergic to the sap.)

This heracleum, a native of North America and western Asia, strikes a note of the theatre – of comedy, not tragedy – when encountered in the wild garden, a backdrop for a children's picnic. It is too coarse a plant for the border, and is not suitable for a small garden, unless you like to try something unusual among shrubs. It will grow in sun or shade, but needs a little moisture, and looks enchanting by a pond. Sow seeds *in situ* in the autumn.

Heracleum mantegazzianum

Iris laevigata

This superlative iris is a true aquatic, growing just as well in shallow water as by the margin of a pond or lake, a gift for masking the hard edge of an artificial garden pool. A native of Japan and China, the smooth spears of pale green leaves make a background for hosts of deep lavender-blue flowers with broad, drooping falls, the whole plant doubly beautiful when reflected in the water. This is a beardless iris some 2 feet (60 cm) tall, flowering in mid-summer and dying down completely in winter.

Iris laevigata, like most aquatics, should be grown in full sun. The sharp leaves contrast well with the rounded foliage of rodgersias, hostas, or the umbrella plant (*Peltiphyllum peltatum*), a planting for rich, acid soil. All these must be by the water's edge, not in the water, as must *Iris kaempferi*. This is a taller relation of *I. laevigata*, with ribbed leaves and flatter

Many irises require really damp conditions. *Iris laevigata*, a beardless species, is happy with its feet in water. In early summer the deep blue flowers are borne on stems 2 feet (60 cm) tall. The leaves are sword-like.

flowers (the falls and standards melting together), in various shades of blue often marked with white.

Iris laevigata has a lovely variegated form, with cream and green striped leaves, and also a white form. It is possible to grow all these forms in a moist border, but this would involve much pointless watering when even a small pool would offer a more sympathetic home.

Iris laevigata

Kalmia latifolia

Kalmia, also known as calico bush or mountain laurel, a native of mountains in the eastern United States, is one of the finest summer-flowering shrubs for gardeners with acid soil. It is a hardy evergreen growing to great heights in the wild, but is usually not more than 6 to 7 feet (1.8 to 2.1 m) tall in the garden, and rather more in spread. The leaves are glossy and pointed, and those at the tips of the branches shelter clusters of rosy pink cup-shaped flowers crimped like calico, with conspicuous white stamens. The clusters are some 4 inches (10 cm) across, tightly crowded with blossom in a good season.

Kalmias are ericaceous and need a cool, moist position in lime-free soil, preferably in light shade, though an open position is acceptable. In a small garden there would

Kalmia latifolia

scarcely be space for more than one specimen, but if they can be planted in groups kalmias give the same massy effect as clumps of rhododendrons. Where there is no shade, a mulch of peat will

The calico bush or mountain laurel, *Kalmia latifolia*, is a summer-flowering evergreen shrub needing lime-free soil and cool conditions. In the garden it usually grows to a height of 6 to 7 feet (1.8 to 2.1 m).

help to keep the roots cool.

Shrub books are careful to warn you that the leaves are poisonous to cattle, but this is a rare hazard, and on the only occasion when cows burst into my garden, I did not wish them well.

Ligularia dentata

Ligularia could not be called a subtle plant in either size or colour, but it has a harsh splendour by the waterside on hot days in the height of summer. It is a herbaceous perennial from China and Japan, making large clumps of toothed leaves which are almost circular. These are beetroot red when they appear in spring; as they mature, growing up to 3 feet (90 cm) in height, the upper sides of the leaves turn bright green, but the undersides remain purple. The dark purple flower stalks later out-top the leaves, branching in summer to bear enormous heads of orange daisy flowers with brown centres, coarse but spectacular; when crowded with butterflies the plant looks very summery indeed. The best-known variety is 'Desdemona', the leaves

'Desdemona' is a compact variety of *Ligularia dentata*, a moisture-loving herbaceous perennial. In this form, the reverse of the leaf remains purple.

deeply flushed with purple underneath and there is another variety called 'Othello'. I cannot myself see any difference between them.

Ligularias must have rich soil and a great deal of moisture and are usually grown in the sun, though some gardeners find that the leaves are more robust in light shade. They must be planted beside the water, but not so near that the crowns are submerged in winter, or they will rot. They can, indeed, be planted on a mound of soil.

Plant 3 feet (90 cm) apart with other water-loving plants which will not be crowded out by its size – *Hosta sieboldiana*, the largest-leaved of our hostas, royal fern (*Osmunda regalis*) and perhaps skunk cabbage (*Lysichitum americanum*), with golden arum flowers in spring. Cornuses and willows, pollarded almost to the ground every year, would provide stems of many colours.

Monarda didyma

Monarda, or bergamot, is a highly aromatic labiate plant which was long ago elevated from the herb garden to the herbaceous border. The first bergamot to be introduced to Britain from its native Virginia in North America was *M. fistulosa*, collected by John Tradescant the younger in 1637 on one of his epic plant-hunting journeys across the Atlantic.

But *M. didyma* is a larger and more brilliant plant, introduced to Britain from Oswego, on Lake Ontario, in 1744. It is sometimes called bee balm, because of its richness in nectar, and sometimes Oswego tea, because it was a favourite herb for making *tisane*. It is a handsome hardy herbaceous perennial, with whorls of scarlet tubular flowers on stalks 2 feet (60 cm) high, which carry hairy, nettle-like, scented leaves all the way up. A curiosity in its growth is that when the first flush of whorls is fading, the stalks grow upwards from the centre for another two or three inches, and a fresh whorl blooms on top, so the flowering season lasts for nearly three months from mid-summer into early autumn.

Monarda didyma

Monarda didyma needs sunshine, but it also demands moisture, and burns up if not watered in dry weather. It also likes a lot of food, and regular mulches will both feed the plant and keep the roots moist. It spreads fast, and though it looks best in bold plantings, the clumps may need dividing every other year in spring.

The best-known variety is 'Cambridge Scarlet', but there are other forms in pink, purple and white. This is an excellent plant to grow with phlox, which like the same rich, moist conditions.

Bergamot, *Monarda didyma*, is a hardy herbaceous perennial with an exceptionally long flowering season, starting in mid-summer. Scarlet labiate flowers are carried on stalks 2 feet (60 cm) high.

The water forget-me-not, *Myosotis scorpioides*, a European evergreen species, bears yellow-centred blue flowers over a long period in summer. It grows 12 inches (30 cm) tall.

Myosotis scorpioides

Many of the plants appropriate for damp places are large, particularly in their leaves, but this charming little native forget-me-not, also known as *M. palustris*, could be grown beside the smallest garden pool. A hardy perennial, it grows up to 12 inches (30 cm) at most, and bears masses of blue forget-me-not flowers with yellow centres in early and mid-summer. A fast grower, it will spread from the verge of the pond into shallow

Myosotis scorpioides

water, making a blue pool of flower on the surface. Being small, it follows that it should be grown with other water-loving plants which will not overwhelm it, such as marsh marigold, or *Caltha palustris*, with a few irises for variety of shape.

Both the forget-me-not and the marsh marigold need boggy, not just moist, soil. Plant the forget-me-nots 12 inches (30 cm) apart.

Rheum palmatum

A fine plant for the back of a well-watered border or for a place of honour beside a pool, the ornamental rhubarb can often be accommodated where the giant *Gunnera manicata* is too large. It is exciting from the moment when the bright cerise leaf-buds push through the soil in early spring. They emerge reddish and crumpled, as though from a laundry wringer, but unfold into noble lobed and dissected leaves, bronze-green with crimson on the underside, some 3 feet (90 cm) across. The stalks are red, too, like those of culinary rhubarb. In early summer, tall spikes rise to 5 feet (1.5 m) in height carrying great panicles of small, creamy flowers. There is a variety, 'Atro-sanguineum', with crimson flowers and dark red, almost black, foliage.

Rheum palmatum is an ornamental rhubarb that is magnificent in flower and leaf. The flower spike, which is generally creamy but can be purple or pink, grows to 5 feet (1.5 m) in early summer.

Rheum palmatum

Rheums should be planted 6 feet (1.8 m) apart in full sun and moist soil enriched with manure, and must not dry out, but neither must the crowns be so wet as to rot in winter. Some gardeners plant them on little mounds of soil to promote good drainage.

Rheums look rather tatty after flowering, and something equally dramatic should be waiting in the wings for late summer, a great opportunity for a group or two of crimson dahlias.

Rodgersia pinnata 'Superba'

Rodgersias are star plants for any garden that can provide a little permanent moisture in the soil. These are herbaceous perennials, which one thinks of first as foliage plants, though the flowers are tall and handsome. *Rodgersia pinnata* 'Superba', a selected form of a Chinese species, has large pinnate leaves, which are bright

Rodgersia aesculifolia

Of the herbaceous perennials, the rodgersias are in the first rank of foliage plants for moist conditions. *Rodgersia pinnata* can grow to 3 feet (90 cm); the form 'Superba' has wonderfully burnished leaves.

bronze. In mid-summer these are out-topped by brilliant pink, feathery flower-heads. The hairy bronze-green fans of another Chinese species, *R. aesculifolia*, look exactly like the leaves of a horse chestnut, and grow well above the ground on stalks that are 2 feet (60 cm) high. The flowers unfurl like ferns in spring and bloom in mid-summer, tall, creamy plumes of star-shaped blossom standing some 2 feet (60 cm) above the chestnut leaves.

Rodgersias like rich, moist, peaty soil and revel in a sunny place by a pond or in

a ditch, but they are adaptable plants. They will grace a damp border and grow well by the house in suitably moist soil, where they benefit from protection from the wind. They will accept lime, and are often grown in light shade. They make excellent ground-cover, and for elegance and beauty more than hold their own among the many other fine plants of the waterside, such as hostas, irises, astilbes, and many more. Plant the rhizomes 30 inches (75 cm) apart in groups of three, five, seven or more, according to the space at your command.

81

The kaffir lily, *Schizostylis coccinea*, is a rhizomatous perennial. In autumn it sends up from among grassy leaves a stem 2 to 3 feet (60 to 90 cm) tall carrying crimson or pink flowers.

provide a pleasant contrast of colour and leaf form. Alternatively, it could be grown in a moist bed with Michaelmas daisies.

Trollius × cultorum

Boggy ground, including the marshy places of northern Britain, is the natural habitat of the beautiful wild globe flower, *Trollius europaeus*, but it, like the larger hybrids, will make its home just as well beside a garden pool.

This species and the hybrids are like large buttercups in flower and leaf, with stalks about 18 inches (45 cm) high, or considerably more in the case of the hybrids. They are an arresting sight, making perfect globes of folded petals in various shades of yellow and orange rising from a mass of bright green, palmate leaves. Plants increase slowly to make large clumps and flower for a long period from early summer.

Plant them 18 inches (45 cm) apart in good, moist soil, perhaps with irises

'Orange Globe' is one of the deep-coloured globe flowers, the moisture-loving species and hybrids of *Trollius*. The leaves are handsomely palmate and most of the hybrids form clumps from 2 to 3 feet (60 to 90 cm) tall.

Schizostylis coccinea

Schizostylis coccinea, or kaffir lily, a native of high, well-watered places in South Africa, is a plant of the iris family which flowers remarkably late in the year, from autumn into early winter. A tall plant from 2 to 3 feet (60 to 90 cm) high, it has swordlike leaves and stems which bear a number of cup-shaped flowers. These open into stars in bright light. The species is scarlet, but there are varieties in other shades of red and pink; 'Major' has crimson satiny flowers, 'Sunrise' is a soft

pink. The plant is hardy except in cold districts, for which it is not suitable, and likes a sheltered place in the sun and a great deal of moisture – the margin of a stream or pool is the nearest thing to its natural home. It lasts for several weeks as a cut flower.

Plant *Schizostylis* in enriched soil, putting in two or three plants 9 inches (23 cm) apart, and keep it moist throughout summer and autumn, mulching in summer with peat. A plant which will still be in flower when the kaffir lily blooms is *Astrantia major*, and a large group would for contrast of form – our native yellow flag (*I. pseudacorus*), or blue *I. sibirica*, with white markings on the falls. If there is space for a shrub in the background, one of the dogwoods would make an ideal choice.

Famous names among the hybrids are 'Canary Bird' and 'Fireglobe'.

Trollius × *cultorum*

Viburnum tomentosum plicatum 'Mariesii'

This spectacular viburnum from China and Japan is a specimen shrub, if ever there was one. Its tiered architectural shape must be seen in splendid isolation, and as its lowest branches sweep the ground there is no question of under-planting. It was introduced into Britain towards the end of the last century by Charles Maries, who collected in the Far East for the nursery firm of Veitch.

The main stems of 'Mariesii' grow some 8 to 10 feet (2.4 to 3 m) high, and from these spring horizontal branches some 7 feet (2.1 m) long, so that the total spread of the shrub in maturity is very wide. The owner of a large garden who wishes to plant a group should space them 12 feet (3.6 m) apart, so that only the tips of the branches will overlap.

'Mariesii' is a plant for all seasons. In early summer every branch will be laden with flat clusters of pure white lacecap flowers, rather like those of a lacecap hydrangea, which last for several weeks. In autumn the oval leaves will turn crimson and the central fertile flowers

will mature into bunches of scarlet berries, and when leaves and berries fall, the bare skeleton of the shrub will still attract attention.

This viburnum is quite easy to grow. It prefers a rich, slightly moist soil, either acid or alkaline, in a sunny position, but is not fussy, and will thrive in a dry soil if watered well when young. Dark, glossy evergreens, such as *Elaeagnus* × *ebbingei* or *Viburnum* × *burkwoodii* (flowering earlier) would make a good background for a single specimen; or a group could be planted beside a pond, in a scenic setting of water and sky.

A very similar shrub listed in most catalogues is the variety 'Lanarth', which is

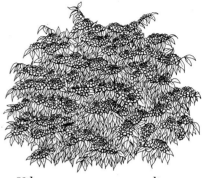

Viburnum tomentosum plicatum
'Mariesii'

equally robust but of a less tabulated structure.

The tiered and spreading branches of *Viburnum tomentosum plicatum* 'Mariesii', a large shrub up to 10 feet (3 m) high, are laden with lace-cap flowers in early summer. In autumn there are scarlet berries.

THE SHADY GARDEN

Rhododendrons and camellias, which are among the finest flowering evergreens that do well in shade, frame a view over a lightly wooded landscape. Although some species and cultivars make large shrubs, there are many others suitable for planting in small gardens.

A foreground of London pride *(Saxifraga umbrosa)*, flanking ferns and a background of *Hydrangea petiolaris* are permanent features of a shady corner lightened in summer by a pot of ivy-leaved geraniums.

dense canopy of evergreens shutting out all the light all the time, but deciduous trees are not a problem, for they will let in the light in winter, and spring plants can grow and flower before the leaves of the trees come out. Sometimes, a stripping of the lower branches will allow more light to penetrate than if a tree is left un-pruned. That great American plantsman, Lanning Roper, was a champion of this method.

Shade-loving plants are by nature woodlanders, and those plants will do best which are related to the shade-loving plants of the wild. The woodland floor under most deciduous trees, parti-cularly oak, is cool and moist, and fed by its own decaying leaves, but though some plants will accept the drier shade of, say, a

RIGHT Bright saxifrages hold the centre stage but in winter and early spring the shade-tolerant hellebores at the foot of shrubs and hedges give this garden another focus of interest over many weeks.

BELOW Lush large-leaved plants and vividly coloured rhododendrons flourish in a moist glade-like setting. Woodland plants, including many fine species, are among the most easily adapted to shady gardens.

Shade has always been prized in the garden, in the cool British Isles as well as in the hot countries of the world. Plants look beautiful in dappled light, and leafy arcades, orchards twittering with the song of birds, woodland glades and sheltering arbours have always been the stuff of poetry. In novels, the shrubbery is a traditional scene for flirtation, and a shady oak or cedar a choice spot for a picnic. The shade of walls or buildings can be equally alluring, and a courtyard or a town terrace can make an attractive home for plants, perhaps enhanced by the trickle of a little fountain. Indeed, ground open to the sky, though enclosed by walls, may get a high concentration of light, so that the town gardener can have flowers as well as greenery. The only shade which defeats the gardener is a

chestnut tree, with crackly leaves which do not rot, they may need the help of an occasional moisture-retaining mulch of leafmould or compost.

Shade-loving plants often have recognizable characteristics. Some, like rodgersias, have evolved large leaves which make the most of the available light. Some, like honeysuckle, are climbers which like their roots in the shade but will not flower until they have reached the sunlight. Ferns are born for shade. So are some of the early spring bulbs, like our native wild daffodils, which Wordsworth saw 'Beside the lake, beneath the trees, Fluttering and dancing in the breeze.'

Though most of the plants in this chapter are happiest in shade, preferably light shade, many are accommodating and will thrive in a sunny spot if it is not too dry; hostas, for instance, will grow almost anywhere, and so will the climbing hydrangea, *H. petiolaris*, some of the daphnes, and many more. Though primroses are typical plants of coppiced woodland, they have sown themselves all over a dry, sunny, unpromising bank in my own garden, so one must never be dogmatic. I think, too, of sunny railway embankments thick with primroses enjoyed from the windows of a train, a habit, I am thrilled to see, which is spreading to motorways. Conversely, some sun-loving plants, like peonies, will grow in shade, and will last much longer than in sunshine. William Robinson commended them as good plants for shady corners.

When planting a shady area, some

BELOW The shady side of walls is often thought to present a planting problem. The self-clinging *Hydrangea petiolaris* is one of several climbers and lax shrubs which are happy on a north wall. This hydrangea is a plant of year-round beauty.

ABOVE Shade-loving woodlanders are generally best planted in an informal way. When a more formal treatment succeeds, as with these hostas, the setting makes a major contribution.

LEFT A wild garden that recaptures the random charm of woodland can be suggested even in a small garden, with ferns and other shade-lovers planted beneath a single tree or a clump of trees and shrubs.

gardeners like to lighten the darkness with golden-leaved or variegated shrubs. Golden privet makes an exciting splash where the common privet would be deadly; variegated ivies are among the best members of their family; the lovely golden philadelphus, *P. coronarius* 'Aureus', prefers shade to sun.

Coming back to the woodland nature of the shady plants, it follows that they look best grown informally — bulbs naturalized, biennials self-seeded, shrubs and perennials in loose groupings. Even in a shady town garden a formal row of plants is risky; getting irregular quantities of light, they might not develop at the same rate.

In general, shade is not a quality to be deplored, but is one of the garden's most attractive assets.

Brunnera macrophylla

This useful hardy perennial is a member of the borage family, and so of good bourgeois stock. An accommodating foliage plant for a wild garden or shady border, it has hairy, heart-shaped leaves which grow very large in the course of the summer and charming sprays of small forget-me-not flowers in spring. It is easy to grow in any soil, but needs shade, for the leaves scorch in hot sun.

The green-leaved *Brunnera* has a more distinguished relative, *B. m.* 'Variegata', with quite beautiful green leaves bordered with creamy white. Like many variegated plants, it grows slowly and needs a little cosseting in the way of extra moisture and an occasional mulch.

Plant *B. macrophylla* in large groups of at least five plants 2 feet (60 cm) apart; they will quickly grow into strong, weed-suppressing clumps, and will also seed round about. This quite ordinary plant has a happy way of enhancing the beauty of surrounding plants, such as lilies, and lends its foliage to flowers without good leaves of their own. I think particularly of some of the late spring bulbs, like bluebells and the richly scented double narcissus 'Cheerfulness', both stiff-stalked creatures which are improved by borrowed greenery at their feet.

The large hairy leaves of *Brunnera macrophylla* form clumps about 18 inches (45 cm) high, topped by blue flower sprays in spring.

Brunnera macrophylla

Camellia 'Donation'

Few plants have inspired such a chorus of praise among gardeners as this superb Camellia. The botanist-nurseryman, Harold Hillier, described it as 'perhaps the most beautiful Camellia raised this century'. It is one of the Williamsii group named after J.C. Williams of Caerhays Castle in Cornwall, who first crossed *C. japonica* (very hardy) with *C. saluensis*

Camellia 'Donation'

(prolific of seed) to produce cultivars which are both hardy and free-flowering. One connoisseur, seeing 'Donation' for the first time, is said to have stood before it taking his hat on and off several times.

'Donation' is, of course, evergreen, with glossy toothed leaves and enormous semi-double flowers up to 5 inches

'Donation' is an outstanding hybrid camellia, forming a handsome shrub up to 12 feet (3.7 m) high clothed with glossy evergreen leaves. It is hardy and flowers very freely in mid-spring.

(12.5 cm) across in a rich pink with a strong tinge of blue. The plant will grow in time up to 12 feet (3.7 m), flowering profusely in mid-spring. If hit by a hard frost, the flowers will fall, but many new buds will open. In really cold districts, it can be grown under glass.

Like all camellias, 'Donation' requires

In planting 'Donation' in the open garden it is important to remember that the colour has much blue in it and swears with salmon pink or red flowers. I have seen it exquisitely planted with white camellias and even pale yellow rhododendrons, and often with later-flowering shrubs like roses or hydrangeas, for thought must be given to the many months when camellias are somewhat sombre evergreens. Lily-of-the-valley, which would normally be in leaf and bud while the camellia is in flower, would make a harmonious underplanting.

Clematis 'Perle d'Azur'

A well-drained, limy soil presents many problems to the gardener, but, by way of compensation, he will have spectacular results with clematis. The large-flowered hybrids are hardy climbers which bloom over an exceptionally long period, some for four or five months, and the choice is wide. One of the most exciting is 'Perle d'Azur', of a colour which is rare in the

Clematis 'Mrs Cholmondeley'

clematis family, sky-blue with scarcely a tinge of mauve, and a succession of flowers from mid-summer for at least eight weeks. 'Mrs Cholmondeley' blooms for even longer, from early summer into autumn, with enormous lavender-blue flowers, but austere critics complain that the sepals are too narrow for perfection. Both these hybrids will grow to 10 feet

(3 m), best, in my view, on trellis, though some gardeners grow them through shrubs, an informal method better suited to the small-flowered species. There are also varieties in all shades of mauve, purple, red, and white, as well as some with striped flowers, like the celebrated mauve-and-lilac 'Nellie Moser'.

These clematis like to flower in the sun, but to have their roots in the shade, so shelter the roots with a ground-cover plant, or with tiles or stones. Clematis will flower over a longer period, and be richer in colour, on an east, west, or even a north wall, rather than on a south wall.

Plant in a large hole with plenty of rotted manure or compost below the roots, work some peat among the roots, and add grit to the soil if it is not naturally well-drained. After planting, cut back the shoots in the first spring to 12 inches (30 cm) from the ground, and prune the summer-flowering hybrids every following spring to 5 feet (150 cm), cutting each stem above a pair of strong buds.

'Perle d'Azur' is one of the finest of the large-flowered clematis hybrids, growing to a height of 10 feet (3 m) and flowering over many weeks from mid-summer. Like others of its kind, it thrives in limy soil.

special cultivation. It likes best to grow under a high canopy of scattered trees, like pine or oak, in acid soil rich in humus; it needs moisture at the roots and good drainage. Being shallow-rooted, it is vulnerable to drying winds, and should be regularly mulched. Having said this, it is heartening to see how many town gardens are enlivened in spring with a few camellias, either in open ground or in tubs of peaty soil, in the northern hemisphere always sited against a north or west wall so that early sunshine will not catch the night frost on the buds.

The scented, waxy flowers are the chief beauty of the lily-of-the-valley, *Convallaria majalis*, but the long-lasting leaves, up to 8 inches (20 cm) high, make dense ground-cover, where it is happy. It can be unpredictable in its preferences.

Convallaria majalis

The lily-of-the-valley, though happy in slightly acid or in alkaline soil, and in either town or country gardens, is a little bit unpredictable. Plant it in ideal conditions and it may not settle; plant it in an unlikely place and it may romp away. Graham Thomas, plantsman extraordinary, suggests planting it 'here and there' to see which site suits best.

A native woodland plant, it was once common in Britain in the wild, and Miss Mitford, author of the nineteenth-century classic, *Our Village*, used to pick it in basketsful in the Hampshire woods.

Convallaria majalis

Geoffrey Grigson, author of the contemporary classic, *The Englishman's Flora*, says that, confounding all expectation, it still grows in dry limestone places in Yorkshire, though it is now increasingly rare. It is still common in France, especially in forests near Paris.

Few flowers have such intensity of scent. Each flower stalk, springing from a pair of large, fresh green elliptical leaves, is 6 to 8 inches (15 to 20 cm) tall, and carries a number of tiny white waxy bells in late spring which pour out a perfume rivalled only by that of sweet-peas. It prefers a light soil rich in leafmould, and when the plant takes kindly to its situation it will spread rapidly underground to form a carpet. Deciduous small trees make a friendly canopy, and it is rampant under an arching cotoneaster in my own chalky cottage garden, though I have seen it thriving just as well under a garden wall in London. I give mine a mulch of compost when the leaves have died down. Do not plant it too closely; crowns put in 6 inches (15 cm) apart will soon join up if they take kindly to their site.

The garden variety 'Fortin's Giant', rather larger than the wild form, flowers a week or two later, so that if you grow both you can have lilies-of-the-valley in bloom for a month on end. They are perfect for picking for a cool room.

Cornus mas

This dogwood, often called cornelian cherry, has three seasons of interest in the year. It is one of the first shrubs to flower in spring, fluffy, pale yellow flowers nestling in clusters on the bare twigs like Easter-egg chickens. In late summer, there is occasionally, after a hot summer, a crop of bright red edible fruits, which are still used in some countries to make preserves and cordials. In autumn, the leaves turn bronze and red and provide a good splash of colour.

Cornus mas, an easy and satisfactory shrub, grows to about 12 feet (3.7 m), more in a mild climate, is deciduous and hardy, and will grow in any good garden soil, with or without lime. It is a late developer, flowering sparsely to begin

Cornus mas

with, but Vita Sackville-West discovered that 'it improves yearly with age and size and one year will suddenly surprise you by the wealth of its blossom.' Once established, it will provide you with plenty of branches for the house to mix with evergreen foliage.

Plant it, if possible, against a dark evergreen background, such as holly, and underplant it with pale yellow crocuses and early daffodils, like 'February Gold'.

Dicentra spectabilis

Colloquially known as bleeding heart, *Dicentra spectabilis* is an exquisite herbaceous plant from Siberia and Japan, with tiny flowers unlike any others in the garden. In early summer, racemes of rosy red heart-shaped lockets, with white petals protruding from the centre, dangle from arching stems about 2 feet (60 cm) tall. The grey-green leaves are particularly fine-cut and feathery.

This *Dicentra* likes a shady, sheltered position in light soil with plenty of humus, and must not be disturbed, for the roots are brittle. Mrs Fish grew drifts of it in front of Solomon's seal in her famous cottage garden in Somerset, counteracting the effects of lime in the soil by good cultivation, for it is not noted as a lime-lover. It was a favourite cottage plant

The cornelian cherry, *Cornus mas*, a deciduous twiggy shrub sometimes more than 12 feet (3.7 m) tall, has curious yellow flowers in spring, sometimes followed by red fruits. The leaves colour well in autumn, giving another season of interest.

Bleeding heart, *Dicentra spectabilis*, has long been a popular cottage plant. This herbaceous perennial grows to 2 feet (60 cm) and its grey-green foliage is a fine complement to the rosy red flowers.

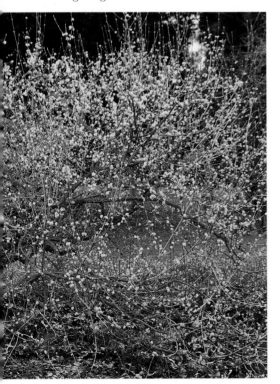

with the Victorians, and in the glorified cottage garden at Sissinghurst Castle is grown with many other herbaceous perennials as underplanting for old-fashioned shrub roses.

Some gardeners find other *Dicentra* species easier to grow, especially *D. formosa* from North America, which makes a ferny mound from which rise mauve-pink flowers of the same heart shape. The variety 'Adrian Bloom' has crimson flowers, and there is a lovely white form, 'Alba', but they have not the curious parti-coloured effect of the red and white *D. spectabilis*.

Digitalis purpurea

The best of all foxgloves is the wild species of British woods and banks – it is almost impertinent to try to 'improve' a plant of such elegance and charm. A hardy biennial, with rosettes of leaves at the base, the flower is too well-known to need lengthy description. It is 3 to 4 feet (90 to 120 cm) tall, with drooping tubes of flowers up one side of the stalk in mid-summer. The flowers are in shades of purple, white, or sometimes a pure and lovely pink, richly spotted inside.

The foxglove is very much a cottage plant, brought in from the wild over many centuries for herbal use, and is one of the few plants still used in modern

Dicentra spectabilis

The elegant spires, up to 4 feet (1.2 m) tall, of the biennial foxglove, *Digitalis purpurea*, look at home in the wild garden and are not to be despised wherever there is light shade. Foxgloves self-seed freely.

medicine, a treatment for heart disease. The cottage paintings of Helen Allingham, a friend of Ruskin, Tennyson and Browning, which now fetch high prices in the saleroom, nearly always have foxgloves waving among the roses and pansies by the cottage door.

There is room for foxgloves in almost every garden which boasts a tree or a few shrubs, for it likes a little shade; it prefers light soil, with some humus. Being biennial, seed should be sown in two successive years to get continuity of flower, after which it will seed itself for ever. The hybrid 'Excelsior' strain, which I deplore, has horizontal flowers clumsily crowded all round the stalk, but there is a pleasant perennial foxglove, *D. grandiflora,* with yellow flowers.

Foxgloves look best scattered among plants as unpretentious as themselves, and the tall, pink-flowered rose species, *Rosa glauca,* with leaves of soft blue-green on red stalks, makes a perfect background. Sow the seeds outdoors in

early summer, preferably *in situ,* for flowering the following year.

Foxgloves require no staking, no feeding, no dosing for disease, and the leaves provide winter ground-cover. What more can any plant be asked to give?

Eranthis hyemalis

The winter aconite is one of the joys of the dark months of late winter, its cheerful little bright yellow buttercup flowers, in their surrounding collars of narrow green leaves, surviving wind and snow without distress. Flowering in a succession, they should provide a show over several weeks. In bloom, the stalks are at most 4 inches (10 cm) high, but after flowering they go on growing up to at least 8 inches (20 cm) and can look untidy unless they are planted in (deciduous) woodland. Alternatively, an island bed makes a good site, with some shrubs for shade and some early summer perennials, like columbines and peonies, to conceal the fading aconites with their

The tuberous-rooted winter aconite, *Eranthis hyemalis*, is a delightful plant for naturalizing. The green-ruffed yellow flowers, at most 4 inches (10 cm) high, give promise of another spring while winter still holds its grip.

Eranthis hyemalis

fresh foliage. But I must not give the impression that aconites need a large space, for a small, shady bed can suit them well, and I have clumps by my own front door to greet the winter guest.

Aconites will grow in almost any soil except heavy clay, and will often prosper in sun – some of the best I have seen are self-sown in a sunny gravel path, where the owners have sensibly left them alone. Once they have 'taken', each corm will in time form a large clump, and they seed themselves generously.

But suppose they fail to take? I am sure this is because the gardener has bought and planted hard, dry tubers in autumn. It is better to plant aconites in spring while still green and growing, and such plants can be bought for an extra price. But surely every gardener has a friend with aconites who will hand over a spadeful soon after flowering? My own plentiful stock has grown from just such a gift made years ago, and reminds me of the giver every spring.

Geranium endressii

The hardy geraniums are the best family of garden plants for providing ground-cover, and next to my beloved *G. macrorrhizum* I would place *G. endressii.* It has a gentle beauty, flowers for many months from early summer, and is easy to control, for it does not try to throttle your star plants, but keeps to its allotted quarters.

Geranium endressii is a hardy herbaceous perennial with small pink flowers

Geranium endressii makes attractive evergreen ground-cover, the deeply lobed leaves forming a mound up to 18 inches (45 cm) high. The pink flowers are carried over a long season.

carried well above the massed light green, deeply lobed leaves. The best variety is 'A.T. Johnson', with pink flowers with a curious metallic sheen. It will grow in any garden soil in sun or shade, but lasts longer in cool conditions.

Being soft in colour, it looks well against a strong, dark background, especially purple. I have seen it in a shady place with *Campanula glomerata,* which has dense clusters of bell flowers round the stalks, and in sun with purple irises and the wine-dark rugosa rose, 'Roseraie de l'Haÿ'.

Plant the geraniums 18 inches (45 cm) apart, and they will soon join to make a weed-suppressing colony.

Geranium macrorrhizum

One of the best of all carpeting plants, this geranium spreads rapidly, but is never invasive. If it exceeds its allotted space, you just pull it up by hand.

A nearly evergreen perennial, its beauty is in the spreading masses of frilly, five-lobed leaves, which are soft green for most of the year, but scarlet in autumn, and when they die away at last, the young leaves are ready and waiting. The leaves are highly aromatic, and it is a joy to crush one and release the scent on a summer's day. The flowers, some 12 inches (30 cm) high, are magenta, but in the attractive form 'Ingwersen's Variety', they are rose-pink.

Geranium macrorrhizum grows equally well in sun or light shade and prefers dry soil, which makes it an excellent ground-cover among greedy shrubs. A very few plants, put in 18 inches (45 cm) apart, will be enough to start with if you want to grow a carpet, for they will quickly join up, and you can pull off pieces, whether rooted or not, on a wet spring day, add them to your group, and they will root. If you have struggled, as I have, with

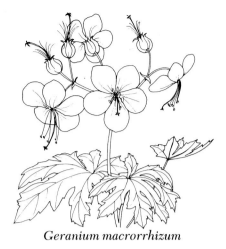

Geranium macrorrhizum

aggressive carpeters, like the lamiums, and wish you had never set eyes on them, you will appreciate this lovely geranium's good behaviour.

Although a vigorous, spreading plant, *Geranium macrorrhizum* does not itself become a weed. The aromatic leaves make a carpet 12 inches (30 cm) high. The flowers are magenta, pink or white.

Helleborus orientalis

The Lenten rose, a lovely plant from Greece and Asia Minor, will tolerate quite deep shade and looks best among shrubs. In my own garden there are a few groups in the shadow of laurels, interspersed with snowdrops, though I prefer them among my airier deciduous shrubs, like *Kolkwitzia amabilis*.

This hellebore is evergreen, with new, deeply cut, exquisite leaves appearing when you cut away the old leaves in autumn. The flowers follow in very early spring and there is a succession over many weeks. These are saucer-shaped and nodding, two or three on each stem, and highly variable in colour, white, green, pink, crimson or purple, the petals speckled inside, the conspicuous stamens creamy-yellow. All are hybrids and cross freely, seeding all over the place, but the young plants should be selected as soon

The lenten rose, *Helleborus orientalis*, produces a succession of flowers in early spring. Each stem, up to 18 inches (45 cm) high, carries two to three flowers ranging in colour from white to deepest purple, some speckled on the inside.

as they flower, for, though you may get an enchanting new colour from your lucky dip, some of the shades may be muddy and will spoil your tapestry.

They like a rich, well-drained soil and

need regular mulching; they enjoy lime. Margery Fish used to plant some in a raised position so that she could look into the speckled saucers without crawling on the ground, but this would be risky in a dry garden with over-sharp drainage.

Helleborus orientalis

They are totally frost-proof. If you go out early after a bitter night the hellebores will have collapsed to the ground, but by midday they will be strong and straight again. I do not pick them for vases, for they wilt in a hot room, but flowerheads

can be cut off and floated in a bowl for table decoration, and will then last well.

A very similar hellebore, though not evergreen, is the deep crimson *H. atro-rubens*, which flowers even earlier – I usually discover a few blooms on Christmas Day.

Hosta sieboldiana

Hostas, or plantain lilies, which come to us from Japan, are among the most beautiful of shade-loving plants, clothing the garden with shapely foliage throughout the summer. *Hosta sieboldiana* is the largest member of this fine family, forming mounds of large, ribbed, glaucous leaves. Spires of white flowers spring from the clumps in late summer, or pale mauve flowers (rather washy) if you choose the variety 'Elegans'. The smaller hostas are just as beautiful, and often have bi-coloured leaves, like *H. crispula*, with wavy dark green leaves edged with white, or *H. fortunei* 'Albo Picta', with yellow leaves splashed with green.

Hostas are paragons of virtue. They are hardy. They will grow in any soil, though they prefer it rich and moist. (On

Almost all the plantain lilies have handsome foliage. *Hosta sieboldiana*, which forms mounds up to 30 inches (75 cm) high of ribbed, glaucous leaves, is one of the finest. The flowers appear in late summer.

96

chalk they should be mulched with leaf-mould). They are total weed suppressors. And in my view, not held by all, they die neatly, turning a golden yellow for about a week in autumn, and then disappearing underground.

They look their best close-planted in drifts, perhaps in front of a shady border, or at the edge of a pool, or in pockets of

Hosta sieboldiana

Hydrangea macrophylla 'Blue Wave' is one of the lace-cap hydrangeas. It forms a bush 5 feet (1.5 m) high and across, which on acid soils bears sky-blue flowerheads in late summer.

soil in a town garden, with their leaves spreading over paving. I have seen them associating happily with all manner of taller plants. Their firm leaves contrast well with feathery astilbes. They are splendid in front of lilies and shrub roses in a cool border. Or you could have a little specialized hosta garden, with drifts of three or four different varieties.

Hostas are caviare to slugs, and slug pellets can be put down in early spring before the leaves push out of the ground. But personally, since I learned that chemical slug baits can actually attract slugs from a hundred yards away, I have stopped using them. Some gravel at strategic places, which slugs cannot cross, is perhaps a better idea.

Hydrangea macrophylla 'Blue Wave'

This is not, I am afraid, a shrub for every gardener, for it needs a rich, moist, acid soil and a woodland site, or perhaps a wide shrub border, but it can be admired by visitors in many large collections. A great dome of a shrub, with a height and

spread of 4 to 5 feet (1.2 to 1.5 m), or even more in a mild climate, it bears flat lace-cap flowers of pure sky-blue in a very acid soil, but lilac or pinkish in a neutral soil. Very alkaline soil is unsuitable. Technically, the lace-cap flowers, some 4 inches (10 cm) across, consist of tiny fertile florets in the centre circled by conspicuous blue sterile florets which give the flower its beauty and colour.

'Blue Wave' flowers over many weeks in late summer and early autumn, and

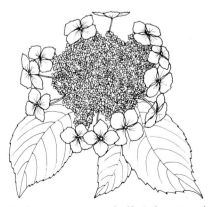

Hydrangea macrophylla 'Blue Wave'

looks best in a natural planting under tall trees, perhaps cypress or pine, though space for a single plant could be found in a sheltered shrub border. It is a bit sprawly for pots, where mophead hydrangeas are perfection. Some gardeners, disappointed with a pinkish tinge in their flowers, dose the plants with alum to increase the acidity, but I view such chemical gardening with distaste. A mulch of peat might blue the flowers in a more natural way.

As a companion in woodland or shrubbery, the male fern, *Dryopteris felix-mas,* is highly compatible. Drifts of bulbs which need acid soil, like erythroniums or trilliums, might be grown for interest in spring.

'Blue Wave' revels in many gardens in Devon, Cornwall, the west coast of Scotland and Wales, Brittany across the English Channel, and other districts with peaty soil; one nearer London is Wakehurst Place, in Sussex, the beautiful country annexe of Kew Gardens, where pools and streams in woodland empty into a large lake. It is open, generously, nearly every day of the year.

and it will climb 60 feet (18 m) up a tree. The great W. J. Bean also suggested growing it as a mound over a tree stump, but (who am I to challenge the master?) I am never happy with climbers in mounds, for tall weeds, like nettles or wild parsnip, always seem to come up through them waving defiantly from impenetrable depths.

Hydrangea petiolaris

Hydrangea petiolaris, sometimes listed under *H. anomala* is a vigorous deciduous climber with aerial roots that allow it to climb to a height of 60 feet (18 m). It flowers freely in mid-summer, even on a shady wall, and the white lacecaps are decorative over a long season.

Hydrangea petiolaris

This is one of the loveliest of climbers if you can give it plenty of space – either the full height of your house, or a sturdy tree with rough bark to which the aerial roots can cling, like those of ivy, for the plant needs no artificial support. Though deciduous, it is a plant of year-round beauty. One of the most cheerful signs of spring is the unfolding of the fresh young leaves, which are later bright green, heart-shaped and deeply toothed. Masses of large, pure white flowers follow in mid-summer, typical hydrangea lacecaps, up to 10 inches (25 cm) across. They remain on the plant for months, looking decorative even when sere, like most hydrangeas. In the darkest months, the network of rich brown branches has its own charm if you have an eye for the skeleton effects of winter.

Hydrangea petiolaris likes good soil, so enrich it generously at planting time, and prefers a north wall to an east or south wall, where morning sun after night frost can cause damage. It grows well on lime, or even chalk. It may not flower for the first two or three years, after which it will climb rapidly. I have seen it growing to the top of a three-storey house, where the only care needed is to prune it round the windows and watch the drainpipes,

Lilium martagon

The Turk's-cap lily is not one of those dramatic lilies with shouting trumpets, but is one of the best for naturalizing if you have a bed of good, deep soil with a few small trees or tall shrubs to provide shade and shelter – the nearest most of us can get to that desirable 'open woodland'. It comes from eastern Europe, grows to about 4 feet (1.2 m) with whorls of leaves up the stalk and small, pinkish-purple spotted flowers with petals so sharply recurved that there is some resemblance to a turban. It is very hardy and will increase in time – it is not one of those unfaithful lilies which seem to be doing so well and then suddenly disappear to cries of 'It must be a virus'. It will grow in sun or part shade in good well-drained soil, with or without lime. The bulbs should be planted in groups 4 inches (10 cm) deep and 9 inches (23 cm) apart.

It flowers in mid-summer and looks well with woodland plants such as foxgloves and ferns. There is a lovely white form, 'Album', which enhances the pink lilies if the two are grown together.

The Turk's-cap lily, *Lilium martagon*, is a graceful woodland bulb with stems about 4 feet (1.2 m) high carrying numerous pendulous flowers in mid-summer. It is an easy plant that is rarely troubled by disease.

Lonicera periclymenum

Lysimachia punctata is a cheerful herbaceous perennial that is too invasive to be put with choice border plants. The yellow spikes, 30 inches (75 cm) tall, brighten rough shady spots.

Lonicera periclymenum

This hardy climber is the honeysuckle, or woodbine, of our woods and hedges, one of the most sweetly scented of all wild flowers. I am usually a champion of flower species in the garden, but in the case of honeysuckle, at least two cultivars have brought gains without losses. The flowers are larger than those of the wild form and the flowering season is longer, and there is no loss of scent.

Early Dutch honeysuckle, *L.p.* 'Belgica', has tubular flowers opening thirstily at the lips, of pale yellow flushed with red, and blooms in early summer and again in autumn. Late Dutch honeysuckle, *L.p.* 'Serotina', flowers from mid-summer, and is more conspicuously red. Both grow to about 15 feet (4.5 m). The leaves of both begin to bud early in the year, and the flowers are followed by red berries, so they interest and charm the gardener over a long period.

Like clematis, honeysuckles do best in rich soil with their roots in the shade and their heads in the sun. Natural twiners, they can be grown on trellis on a wall, but it is more in their nature to scramble through trees and shrubs. Also, they are martyrs to greenfly when confined to a sunny wall, but are less afflicted in airy or shady conditions.

A cottage plant for many centuries, honeysuckle looks best in unsophisticated company, perhaps with hawthorn or musk roses, with simple annuals, like nasturtiums, round the roots.

Early Dutch honeysuckle, *Lonicera periclymenum* 'Belgica', is a fine selected form of the simple woodbine. It is a bushy grower to 15 feet (4.5 m) and flowers in early summer and again in autumn.

Lysimachia punctata

This is not a connoisseur's plant, but I am rather fond of it. In mid-summer it sends up a mass of leafy spikes 30 inches (75 cm) tall with whorls of bright yellow, star-like flowers up the top half of each one. Too brash in colour for the herbaceous border, it makes a delightful pool of yellow in a background of shade.

A hardy herbaceous perennial, this *Lysimachia*, which is related to our native creeping Jenny, prefers moist or even boggy soil, but I have grown it in full sun with perfect success. It is very invasive, not much more than a pretty weed, but you can pull it out in spadefuls in the autumn to keep it under control.

Plant in any soil no closer than 2 feet apart, for the roots will join up underground within a single season, and five plants will take you a long way. It looks well with the largest-leaved hosta, *H. sieboldiana*, but is not strictly a plant for thoughtful association. Just put it in any patch of ground where you want a cheerful filler.

Nandina domestica

This graceful Chinese shrub, the heavenly bamboo, is not a true bamboo, but a member of the berberis family. It makes an evergreen thicket of unbranched stems covered with long, pinnate leaves divided into delicate, pointed leaflets, and is usually grown close to the house for shelter, as E.A. Bowles grew it in his famous garden at Myddelton House, near London. 'In Japan', wrote Mr Bowles, 'every garden, however small, possesses a specimen close by the door'. But this was not so much for its beauty, he explained, rather knocking the poetry out of the conception, as for its aromatic wood, which was ideal for toothpicks. His own plant was 5 feet (150 cm) high, and beautiful all the year round, 'most especially when the young leaves are every imaginable shade of crimson, copper, and bronze, and contrast with the deep green old ones'. In summer he enjoyed the long panicles of white flowers close to the morning-room window, and in autumn the purplish tinge taken on by all the foliage, and the fruit, which sometimes ripens.

Nandina domestica was for long considered too tender for the open garden, but is now found to be hardy in most parts of Britain if given a sheltered position. It is grown in the Rock Garden at the Royal Horticultural Society garden at Wisley, in Surrey, where the climate is

Nandina domestica

The fruits of *Nandina domestica* only ripen in exceptionally favourable years. The evergreen foliage of this shrub, which grows to 6 feet (1.8 m), is reddish when young and turns purplish in autumn.

far from mild, with the protection of tall conifers in the background. It needs good lime-free soil and a shady place, and is well worth trying if the gardener is prepared to take a risk for the pleasure of growing something special.

Pieris japonica 'Blush'

There are several lovely species of the evergreen shrub *Pieris*, but I have chosen *P. japonica* in the variety 'Blush' because it obviates a few difficulties. The species flowers best, but has poor foliage, in the sun, and flowers only sparsely in the shade. In light shade, 'Blush' produces both flowers and leaves of fine quality, and will win some protection from frost. It makes a dense plant and will grow 9 to 10 feet (2.7 to 3 m) high.

It flowers in early spring in glorious drooping sprays of waxy pink flowers resembling lily-of-the-valley. Soon after flowering the shrub begins to put out young bronzy leaves, which turn to polished dark green as they mature. In other species, the foliage is more brilliant, especially in the Chinese *P. formosa* 'Forrestii', which is perhaps the best-known of the genus, but is not so hardy. It flowers in late spring, with sprays of white waxy flowers.

All *Pieris* need the same conditions as rhododendrons, that is, lime-free soil dressed with peat or leafmould, and some shade and shelter. Their seedpods

Pieris japonica 'Blush', an evergreen shrub that grows to 10 feet (3 m), flowers profusely in spring. The young foliage is bronzy rather than brilliant red, as it is in some species and varieties.

should be clipped off in autumn. They can be grown as single plants, but look marvellous massed, and those, like myself, with a garden unsuitable for ericaceous plants, can enjoy the spectacle in one of the great woodland gardens in which Britain is so rich, such as Wakehurst Place, in Sussex, or the Valley Gardens, Windsor, in Berkshire.

Pieris japonica 'Blush'

Primula polyanthus

The multi-flowered primrose, a cross between a primrose and a cowslip, is a very old cottage plant, though coloured forms are not named in garden literature until the middle of the seventeenth century. By the end of the next century, breeding new forms had become a craze with specialist gardeners, or 'florists', and there were many hundreds of named varieties.

Today it is difficult, though not impossible, to find the older, cottage forms of polyanthus, which have been ousted by the modern Pacific hybrids, a giant strain with larger, longer-lasting flowers in a wider range of colours, including a hectic blue, and taller, stronger stalks. The only loss is of charm.

Polyanthus flower in mid-spring, and are natural companions for scillas, grape hyacinths, early tulips and other spring bulbs. They can be grown as biennials from seed, or as perennials, when they must be divided at least every other year and replanted with leafmould. They need rich, moist soil and some shade, for they wilt in full sun, and look attractive planted three or four ranks deep as an edging to a flower-bed or beside a shady path. On a larger scale, they can be grown under small trees, as Miss Jekyll grew them in her garden at Munstead Wood, where they made a Persian carpet in a grove of cob-nuts. Even with the best care in the world, polyanthus may tire of their situation after several years and sicken, and no replenishment of soil will coax them back to health. This phenomenon is known as 'primula sickness', and a new colony must be started in another place. Plant them 12 inches (30 cm) apart.

Cottage gardeners have long cherished the polyanthus, which is derived from the wild primrose. Flower clumps of the old-fashioned varieties stand about 6 inches (15 cm) high but the newer strains are larger.

RHODODENDRON SPECIES AND CULTIVARS

Rhododendrons form a very large genus, the richest source of species being the Himalayas and west China, though many come from other parts of the world. A few introductions to Britain were made some centuries ago, but the great flood of discovery belongs to this century, when such collectors as George Forrest and Frank Kingdon Ward explored 'the eaves of the world'.

Over 500 species and thousands of cultivars are grown in our gardens today, and since all, both the evergreen and the deciduous shrubs, like the same conditions, I will give a brief account of their needs, before choosing a handful of beauties to recommend, selected after observation and discussion with experts, for, regrettably, my own experience is negligible.

Many rhododendrons grow in the wild in very high places in swirling mists and rain-cloud, nearly always in acid soil. It follows that in gardens they like to grow in cool, moist conditions, in light, fibrous acid soil – they do not prosper in clay and lime is poison to them. A woodland situation is ideal, but not dense woodland. Open glades with scattered oak or pine trees make a perfect setting, and give protection from frost. Luckily, many rhododendrons have proved highly adaptable and will grow in ordinary garden conditions, even in sun at a pinch, and do well in town gardens. The leaves are resistant to air pollution, and a building will protect against the biting blast of east winds.

Rhododendrons should be copiously mulched with peat, leafmould, decayed bracken and other non-alkaline organic material. The plants should not be dug or hoed, for they are shallow-rooting and dislike disturbance, and being dense down to the ground, they suppress weeds. They should be deadheaded, if the bushes are not too huge to make this practicable, by cutting close to the faded flower without damaging the bud beneath. They need little pruning. The plants should be kept moist with mulching rather than watering, unless the gardener has a supply of lime-free water, now an increasingly rare asset.

Rhododendron 'Dora Amateis'

This splendid dwarf rhododendron was bred in 1958 in the United States, and is already becoming one of the most widely grown plants in the genus. Free-flowering and hardy, it is a white-flowered hybrid of an American species, *R. carolinianum,* which is exceptionally vigorous, and the Himalayan *R. ciliatum,* a compact, dome-shaped bush with bell-shaped flowers and bristly leaves. The white blooms of 'Dora Amateis' are lightly spotted with green, and come out at the peak of spring.

This hybrid grows best in moist places, where it can be interplanted with lilies, meconopsis, primulas, ferns and other plants which enjoy a damp acid soil. Though the flowers are resistant to frost the plant needs shelter from strong winds. Rhododendron experts assure me

'Dora Amateis' is a dwarf, evergreen rohdodendron that grows to 5 feet (1.5 m). It is fully hardy but should be given protection from fierce winds. It flowers very freely in mid-spring, green spots tinting the white.

that, given this protection, 'Dora Amateis' is among the easiest, as well as the most profusely flowering, of all the white rhododendrons.

Rhododendron luteum

One of the best-loved and most widely grown of the whole genus of rhododendrons, *R. luteum,* formerly known as *Azalea pontica,* is a superlative shrub with many trusses of yellow funnel-shaped flowers and an incomparable scent. A native of the Caucasus, it is deciduous, vigorous, growing usually to about 8 feet (2.4 m) high and 5 to 6 feet (1.5 to 1.8 m) wide, and prodigal of

In late spring *Rhododendron luteum* carries numerous trusses of sweetly scented flowers. In autumn the leaves colour brilliantly. This deciduous species grows to 8 feet (2.4 m).

flowers in late spring. As if this were not enough, it provides a blaze of autumn colour when the leaves turn crimson, purple and orange before they fall. It is the parent of a number of fine hybrids, many of which have been bred in the United States. It is an adaptable plant and one of the easiest rhododendrons to grow, tolerating full sun if need be, and often producing self-sown seedlings.

Rhododendron luteum is a lovely plant to grow in masses in open woodland, together with some of its hybrids, when the scent will carry far and wide, but a single plant in a town garden will give great pleasure, protected from north and east winds by the house.

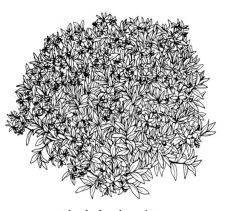

Rhododendron luteum

These rhododendrons look particularly charming with blue flowers planted round about, one species, such as bluebells, to coincide with the flowers in spring, and another with the bright leaves in autumn. At Sissinghurst, a bank of *R. luteum* and other azaleas is planted with blue and white forms of the autumn-flowering willow gentian, *Gentiana asclepiadea*. Lilies bloom among the shrubs in mid-summer.

Rhododendron racemosum

This species would be an excellent choice for a gardener growing rhododendrons for the first time. It is not only one of the prettiest of the smaller rhododendrons, but it is exceptionally hardy, an evergreen shrub up to 5 feet (1.5 m) in height, but usually less. The funnel-shaped flowers are pale pink, though varying in the depth of colour, and grow in clusters along the branches, not at the tips, so that the whole plant is massed with bloom in spring. The admirable French missionary, Père Delavay, was the first collector, sending seeds to Paris in 1889 from west China, where it grows in high mountains, usually as undergrowth in woodland.

There is a dwarf form with cerise pink flowers for the rock garden called 'Forrest's Dwarf', which George Forrest, collecting in 1921, described as 'the finest form I have yet seen'.

Rhododendron racemosum is an evergreen species with glossy, grey-green leaves. It grows to 5 feet (1.5 m) and in spring the shrub is covered with clusters of funnel-shaped flowers.

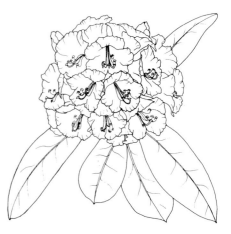

Rhododendron yakushimanum
'Hydon Dawn'

'Hydon Dawn' is one of the many fine hybrids derived from *Rhododendron yakushimanum*. Most have the compact, domed habit of the parent, and rarely grow more than 3 feet (90 cm) high.

Rhododendron yakushimanum

This exquisite rhododendron has a romantic origin. It grows wild in only one place in the world, a small Japanese island called Yaku Shima, which is mountainous, windy and rain-sodden. The species varies according to the altitude of its home, but the plant we grow is a dwarf shrub, a compact shallow dome some 30 inches (75 cm) high and 3 feet (90 cm) wide, the ideal rhododendron (for it has adapted to pleasanter climates) for a small garden.

The evergreen leaves are long, narrow and glossy, but before they develop the young shoots are bright silver; the leaves emerge covered with buff-coloured felt, and when the upper sides turn green, the undersides remain brown and woolly. The flowers of the species also evolve through several interesting stages. The plant produces a multitude of trusses which are rose-pink in the bud, opening to shallow cups of apple-blossom pink, which change to white. The plant has not only compactness of shape and beauty of flower and leaf, but is also hardy and reliable, flowering in equal abundance every year.

In the past few decades, hybrids have been developed from *R. yakushimanum*, and there will be many more. One of the most beautiful is 'Hydon Dawn', with frilled flowers in pure pink and creamy down on the young leaves.

Saxifraga umbrosa

This saxifrage, commonly known as London pride, is a rock plant from the Pyrenees, and by its nature looks most at home in the garden near stone or brick. Like other members of the huge saxifrage genus, it has beautiful leaves. Flat rosettes form an evergreen carpet from which rise tremulous panicles of pink-and-white flowers in early summer. The rosettes spread at a great pace, so that four or five plants, put in 12 inches (30 cm) apart, will soon form a mat of ground-cover. New rosettes can be gent-

Saxifraga umbrosa

ly pulled off and replanted in late summer, preferably in wet weather.

London pride is equally appropriate for large or small areas. I have seen it in a tiny London garden spreading from a small rosebed on to a cobbled path. I have seen it in the country climbing over sarsen stones by a cottage door. On a panoramic scale, it is perfection at Cranborne Manor, in Dorset, where it forms a wide sash on either side of a long path of mellow brick. Cranborne Manor is a splendid Elizabethan house where John Tradescant, one of the early European plant-hunters in North America, is said to have been a gardener three hundred and fifty years ago.

As its name implies, this saxifrage likes shade and will put up with poor soil so long as it is not too dry. When the flowers have faded, pick off the dead stalks in handfuls, and you still have your carpet of rosettes.

There is a good variegated form of *S. umbrosa* with green-and-yellow leaves, and a dwarf form, *S. u. primuloides* 'Elliott's Variety', with rose-red flowers no more than 4 inches (10 cm) tall.

The foam flower, *Tiarella cordifolia*, is a carpeting evergreen perennial with hairy leaves which turn coppery in autumn. It flowers in late spring, the feathery panicles standing about 9 inches (23 cm) high.

The rosettes of evergreen leaves produced so freely by London pride, *Saxifraga umbrosa*, make close ground-cover. Stems up to 12 inches (30 cm) high carry the airy flower panicles in early summer.

Tiarella cordifolia

This species of *Tiarella,* or foam flower, a native of the eastern United States, makes a soft, fresh-looking ground-cover for an airy shrub bed where the shade is light. It is a rampant evergreen perennial, carpeting the earth with pale green, hairy leaves, lobed like maple leaves, which turn coppery in autumn. The tiny white flowers grow in fluffy panicles about 9 inches (23 cm) tall and bloom in masses in late spring.

Tiarella cordifolia likes much the same conditions as another ground-covering member of the saxifrage family, London Pride, that is, a cool place, well-drained soil with some humus, and a little shade. Put in the plants 12 inches (30 cm) apart and they will send out underground runners from which new leaves will shoot to fill in the carpet.

Another somewhat similar saxifrage can claim a place as good evergreen ground-cover, *Heuchera sanguinea*, or coral bells, with panicles of red, pink or white flowers in early summer and handsome marbled leaves. This plant forms clumps rather than a solid carpet, and the roots tend to lift out of the ground. If this happens, the clumps have to be lifted and replanted; as a labour saver, *T. cordifolia* is a better choice.

Tiarella cordifolia

Viburnum tinus

This winter-flowering viburnum is a dream shrub for the small garden, making a dense, round bush of glossy evergreen leaves. The tight clusters of flowers are pink-budded, opening to white from late autumn to early spring. Like box or bay, it strikes the note of formality which a town or courtyard garden needs. The type is 8 feet (2.4 m) tall or more, about the same in width, but the excellent variety 'Eve Price' is smaller, and perhaps better for gardens of limited space.

Better known, perhaps, as laurustinus, its older name, this shrub has been inexplicably out of fashion since an Edwardian heyday, but today gardeners are scrambling to get good plants. A shrub of the Mediterranean, its hardiness was once considered suspect, but it is

Viburnum tinus

reliable in most parts of Britain if given a sheltered place, perhaps against a west wall. It can also be grown under glass. It is lime-tolerant, will grow in sun or light shade, and is particularly successful near the sea. It is a favourite churchyard plant,

Laurustinus, *Viburnum tinus*, is an evergreen, winter-flowering shrub that grows to about 8 feet (2.4 m), though some varieties are more compact. It has a long flowering season and is good for cutting.

The evergreen leaves of *Viola cornuta* make a ground-covering mat, over which the spurred flowers are carried in great number on stems up to 10 inches (25 cm) high. All colour forms are desirable.

often grown in the shelter of the west porch, where it gives the church-goer a pleasant welcome on a winter Sunday. Since the parson was by tradition the best gardener in the village, there is much to be learned from churchyard planting, an interesting subject overdue for research.

Viburnum tinus cuts beautifully, and in warmth gives out a faint, sweet scent.

Viola cornuta

Those who love the innocent faces of wild violets will be enchanted with this species from the Pyrenees, a perfect plant for garden ground-cover. The pale lavender, deep violet or white flowers are spurred and their five petals are somewhat separated, unlike those of big garden pansies. They grow in masses in

border, for they are not appropriate for formal grouping. Keep them watered in dry weather, and shear them over after flowering, following up with a liquid feed to encourage fresh leaves and a later crop of flowers. They increase fast and keep down weeds.

It is difficult to see how anyone could dislike *V. cornuta*, but John Ruskin, always a contradictious critic, described it as a disorderly flower with a lanky flower-stalk 'like a pillar run thin out of an iron-foundry for a cheap railway station'. This is not the only time when Ruskin's eccentric views on flowers have made me grind my teeth.

Viola labradorica

Its provenance proves its hardiness – this brave little violet is a native of Greenland and the most northern regions of America. A low, fast-spreading, ground-cover plant, its chief beauty is in the leaves, which are purple and perpetual. The flowers are much like English dog-violets, perhaps a little smaller, purple and slightly spurred. Abundant in spring, there are occasional flowers all the year round.

This viola will grow in tight clumps in any well-drained soil, in sun or light shade (in deep shade the leaves tend to be green rather than purple), carpeting the ground and seeding almost too freely. It is too dwarf for the mixed border, but makes attractive pools of colour in a rosebed; or dot single plants in a small flowerbed among polyanthus, anemones, muscari and all the bright flowers of early spring.

It is perhaps a shame to give so humble a job to so pretty a plant, but if you have, like most of us, a really horrid corner of your garden where nothing seems to thrive, perhaps near voracious conifers, *V. labradorica* will almost certainly take over and carpet the soil. Put in your plants 12 inches (30 cm) apart.

early summer, rising to about 10 inches (25 cm) from clumps of bright green, toothed, evergreen leaves.

Viola cornuta grows in damp, sunny meadows in the wild, but, unless you can produce similar conditions in your garden, it is better to plant it in light shade, for it cannot endure drought. Put in the plants 12 inches (30 cm) apart in soil rich in humus, and allow them to run about among moisture-loving plants in bed or

Viola labradorica is a very hardy perennial violet, its evergreen leaves, which are purplish, making close ground-cover. The small dark flowers stand about 4 inches (20 cm) high.

Viola cornuta

THE DRY
SHADY GARDEN

Take a walk through a beechwood at almost any time of year, scuffing through the layers of fallen leaves, and count up the number of plants you can find growing on the woodland floor. It will be meagre. Ivy, brambles, half-starved hollies and various primitive mossy things which seem to have missed out on evolution will be the main vegetation. The shallow-rooting trees are too greedy and their shade is too dense for many plants to find a living.

But there are always exceptional plants which grow in a difficult habitat, and you may be rewarded on your walk by occasional spurge laurel, ferns, sweet woodruff, wild arum, white helleborine or stinking iris which have made a home in the dry shade. It is the same in the garden. Dry shade is the least promising of all gardening conditions, but a few plants will succeed there, and I have suggested some of the most promising in the following section.

Dry shade is, of course, a variable condition. The dry shade under buildings is usually easier to plant than the dry shade of trees and shrubs. A shady courtyard can be a delightful oasis, and a bed under the north wall of a house will provide a good home for plants if you choose them well. The advantage of this kind of dry shade is that you can improve the soil. If you work in plenty of humus before you plant, and mulch regularly in later years with compost, manure, peat, leafmould, or whatever other good organic material you can get, the bed

LEFT Dry shady conditions of the kind often found under leafy trees suit the exquisitely beautiful autumn-flowering *Cyclamen hederifolium*.

ABOVE Plants that provide dense ground-cover, such as the thick-leaved bergenias, are among the most valuable for dry shady conditions.

109

will remain shady but you can make it less dry, and unless you are trying to make a garden between two skyscrapers, there should be enough light for the plants to thrive.

The dry shade of trees and shrubs is a different matter. Heavy evergreens are difficult to underplant, especially conifers, but deciduous trees and shrubs give better prospects. Again, you can improve the conditions. You may be able to trim tree or shrub branches to let in more light, as already suggested in a previous introductory section, and of the conifers, the Scots pine can be a hospitable shade-giver if the lower branches are stripped. Also, you can put in your plants with lots of organic matter to give them a good start. But the most important thing is to choose well, and never to force a plant against its nature. Some of the plants I suggest positively like dry shade, others would be more luxuriant with more moisture, but all have a good chance of succeeding in an awkward corner, or on a dry bank, or under the dreaded sycamore in a town garden on which some bureaucratic clown has slapped a Preservation Order.

Arum italicum 'Pictum'

Arum italicum 'Pictum'

This beautiful and interesting herbaceous foliage plant turns the normal seasons of the year upside down. The exciting leaves start to unfold in autumn, and grow larger all through winter and spring, reaching as much as a foot in length. They are shaped like an arrowhead, dark green heavily marbled with very pale green, and waved at the edges. The pale green flowers, which are short and inconspicuous, consist of a spike cloaked in a spathe (a large, enfolding bract) like those of the wild arum, lords and ladies, of the hedgerows. By mid-summer, flowers and leaves have disappeared underground, but in early autumn, spikes of bright red, poisonous berries shoot up like danger signals before the leaf cycle starts afresh.

Arum italicum is hardy in all but the coldest gardens, and will grow in quite deep shade under trees. It prefers a moist place with natural leafmould, but will tolerate dry shade if planted with plenty of moisture-holding compost and peat. The tubers should be planted in summer, 4 inches (10 cm) deep and 9 inches (23 cm) apart, continuing the topsy-turvy calendar followed by this plant. The winter leaves make a perfect backdrop for snowdrops, hellebores or aconites, and are highly prized for winter flower arrangements.

Bergenia cordifolia

Miss Gertrude Jekyll, high priestess of the foliage cult, made lavish use in the gardens she designed of *Bergenia*, then known as *Megasea*. She used bergenias in large drifts of ground-cover 'running back here and there among taller plants'. She planted them in long ribbons to soften the hard edge of paving. She picked the coloured leaves in winter to arrange in bowls with Christmas roses or forced hyacinths, for she gave much thought to flowers in the house.

The marbled leaves of *Arum italicum* 'Pictum' are the plant's beauty in the winter months, their arrowheads standing about 12 inches (30 cm) high. In autumn, there are no leaves but spikes of bright red berries.

Bergenia cordifolia 'Purpurea'

Bergenia cordifolia 'Purpurea', a hardy perennial of the saxifrage family, is, indeed, a great carpeting plant, especially in winter, when the round, leathery, evergreen leaves are suffused with purple. It flowers in spring with (I regret to say) rather gaudy clusters of magenta bells on top of thick red stalks. Even Miss Jekyll admitted that the flowers were coarse, 'but the leaves more than compensate'. There are other bergenias with pink, white or purple flowers and a variety of winter leaf colouring. *Bergenia crassifolia* has perhaps the most exciting leaves; they are crinkly and grow upright, revealing their red-veined backs as well as the upper surfaces of rich red and

The leathery evergreen leaves of *Bergenia cordifolia* 'Purpurea' become purplish in winter. The magenta flowers, which appear in spring, are carried on red stems up to 2 feet (60 cm) high.

mahogany. The flowers are light pink. Both are natives of Siberia of infamous reputation, but I have read in Russian memoirs that the scenery and the flowers are superb when the cruel winter is past.

Bergenias will thrive almost anywhere except under greedy trees or shrubs, but they grow well in the dry shade of walls or buildings. Small pieces planted 12 inches (30 cm) apart will clump up to form a solid carpet impervious to weeds.

Cyclamen hederifolium

This little cyclamen is a native of dry woods in the Mediterranean – I have seen it so massed in a copse in northern Italy that one had to pick a careful path among the plants. The exquisite pink flowers with laid-back petals perch like butterflies on short stalks which grow from flat corms. These are tiny in youth, growing larger every year until, in healthy old age, they look like tea-plates. The cyclamen flower in autumn, and, as they die, each stalk coils like a spring back on to the corm, scattering its seeds, and the famous dark green leaves appear, ivy-shaped and marbled in silver, the pattern varying from plant to plant. They remain evergreen through the winter, a great attraction in the leafless months, and die away in late spring.

This cyclamen is quite hardy and easy to grow in well-drained soil, whether acid or alkaline, in a dry, shady place. Plant the corms, which must be pot-grown, not

Cyclamen hederifolium

bought dry in packets, just below soil level, 6 inches (15 cm) apart, whenever available (probably in spring) under deciduous trees or shrubs, which will allow them summer shade and winter sunlight. I have seen them in pink drifts under an

Cyclamen hederifolium flowers in autumn, the pink or white shuttlecocks carried on stems about 4 inches (10 cm) high. There is a long season through winter and spring of beautifully marbled foliage.

oak tree, in another garden under a larch, and, in Mrs Margery Fish's cottage garden in Somerset, making a pink ribbon in the shade of a hedge.

When the leaves die down, mulch the cyclamen with leafmould, and when seedlings appear near the corms, as they will in plenty, pot them up and keep them under glass for a year for their own safety. If you have no glass, many will survive in the open, but birds, mice and slugs are their enemies in babyhood. Mrs Fish also propagated cyclamen by the rash method of cutting corms into pieces, each one of which would grow.

A lovely pure white form, 'Album', flowers rather earlier than the pink form, and does not seed so freely.

The male fern, *Dryopteris filix-mas*, is a very hardy species that, unlike most ferns, tolerates quite dry conditions. The fronds will grow to a height of 3 or 4 feet (90 to 120 cm), unfurling quickly to make green sprays.

Dryopteris filix-mas

I once bought from a reliable firm a collection of ferns for dry shade, and I planted them in dry shade. Only one succeeded, the inestimable *Dryopteris filix-mas*. This, the true male fern, is not just a filler for an awkward spot in the garden, but is a very beautiful plant indeed. It is a British native, widely distributed in woodlands, preferring some moisture, when it will grow 3 to 4 feet (90 to 120 cm) high, but willing to make a home in dry shade if planted with plenty of humus, though it may not make so large a plant.

In spring, the fronds of the fern appear above the ground curled up like snails. These unfurl quickly and within a month have swelled into rich green sprays of pinnate leaves growing in all directions from the centre, like a fountain. The shape of the plant is so perfect that it is a pity to let side shoots develop, making a formless clump. If possible, cut them away, leaving a single crown, or divide the

plant from time to time. By mid-summer, masses of brown spores appear on the under surface of the fertile leaves, but some leaves are barren, and will be a brighter green. In autumn the plant dies down, but in a wet season it will remain green almost into winter.

Like most ferns with divided leaves, this *Dryopteris* reveals its beauty best if grown in isolation, or several plants can be scattered a few feet apart, perhaps in a carpet of ivy, or other ground-cover with low, uncompetitive foliage.

Ferns were enormously popular with Victorian gardeners, then suffered a decline, but today, when foliage is again as highly prized as flowers, they are enjoying a major revival.

Epimedium × versicolor 'Sulphureum'

Like some exquisite little ballet dancer, this epimedium looks ethereal but is immensely tough. The plant is delicately

Epimedium × versicolor 'Sulphureum'

beautiful in leaf and flower, but makes strong, weed-proof ground-cover. Ideally, I would plant it in a shady spot with some moisture in the soil, but dry, shady places are so difficult to plant, and epimediums will grow in them, that I am suggesting them for these conditions. Occasional mulches of leafmould or compost will supply humus and preserve the scarce moisture.

The epimediums rank among the finest herbaceous plants for ground-cover. *Epimedium × versicolor* 'Sulphureum' forms clumps about 12 inches (30 cm) high of heart-shaped leaves. The flowers are yellow.

A nearly-evergreen hardy perennial, this hybrid slowly forms dense clumps of leaves about 12 inches (30 cm) high. These are the chief attraction, for they are of charming form, toothed and heart-shaped, and change colour through the year, being fresh green in spring, when they are very small, changing to bright green as they expand, and to bronze in autumn. In winter they turn brown and dry, but are usually left on the plant until early spring to protect the flowers from frost. As soon as you detect flower buds in the heart of the clumps, shear the leaves away, or the flowers will be buried in old foliage, and watch the slender stems grow until they are topped with sprays of tiny yellow flowers, spurred like columbines.

Plant them, if you are condemning them to a dry place, with plenty of compost or leafmould, the planting distance depending on whether or not you are impatient for ground-cover. If you are, plant them 12 inches (30 cm) apart and be prepared to divide them after two or three years; otherwise I suggest 2 feet (60 cm) apart, and leave them in peace for a long time.

There are other delightful epimediums with red, pink or white flowers and varying leaf colour in autumn.

Helleborus foetidus

This winter-flowering perennial is one of the greatest of all evergreens, a beautiful plant every day of the year. In early winter it shows promise of the colours to come, a rare combination of pale green with very dark green, for then the pale

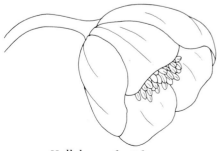

Helleborus foetidus

Helleborus foetidus, which grows to about 2 feet (60cm), is a herbaceous perennial for all seasons. In winter the green flowers contrast with the almost black, deeply divided leaves.

flower buds begin to break away from their sheath of bracts, while the leaves, deeply cut into long, tapering fingers, are so dark that they are almost black. In the following weeks, the buds slowly swell, and by late winter have burst their covering to reveal crowded, drooping clusters of bell-shaped, light green flowers usually rimmed with purple. These will continue to expand over months, and are still decorative when the seed pods have formed. When at last you cut down the flowering stems, the dark green basal leaves cover the ground until the cycle

starts again. The mature plant is up to 2 feet (60 cm) tall.

Helleborus foetidus, which is widely distributed in Europe, will grow almost anywhere, so long as it has good drainage, and will tolerate dry shade. I have seen it most often in the wild in open woodland (though sometimes on chalk cliffs) and think it looks best among deciduous shrubs, perhaps winter-flowering ones, like the yellow, scented Chinese witch hazel, *Hamamelis mollis*.

Plant this hellebore in random groups, not less than 2 feet (60 cm) apart.

Iris foetidissima

This iris will succeed in deep shade and dryish, but not totally arid, soil. It is a fine foliage plant making tall, fan-shaped clumps of glossy green leaves. The mauvish flowers are poor creatures, but they form seed pods which split in autumn to disclose rows of bright orange seeds, so there is beauty and interest all the year round. The plant is named *foetidissima* because it exhales a horrid smell if bruised but, as I am not in the habit of bruising my irises, it has not offended me.

The leaves being spiky, this iris looks best with round-leaved or creeping plants round about. I have seen it planted at random under an oak-tree with bergenias and periwinkles, and it looks splendid, if the soil is not too dry, with one of my favourite euphorbias, *E. amygdaloides robbiae*. Most of us cannot boast an oak-tree in the garden, and I find that of all the trees suitable for smaller gardens, hazels are the most sympathetic to underplanting. The iris is not long-lived,

In autumn and winter the pods of bright seeds are a striking feature of *Iris foetidissima*. The fans of glossy leaves, up to 18 inches (45 cm) tall, make a useful contrast against softer foliage. This iris will do well even in deep shade.

so look for seedlings round about your plants and protect them carefully.

A variegated form of this iris, 'Variegata', with green-and-white striped leaves, needs more light than the plain green species. It is beautiful in winter against low evergreen shrubs, such as skimmias, perhaps with a few early daffodils, like 'February Gold', to make a green, white and yellow picture. It does not bear seeds.

Iris foetidissima

Jasminum nudiflorum

Some plants are ubiquitous, but so satisfactory that they never look stale. Winter jasmine is one, a deciduous, extremely hardy shrub from China smothered in small, starry, yellow flowers on bare stems which illumine dark corners of the garden for most of the winter months. It thrives in any aspect or soil, in country or

Jasminum nudiflorum

The winter-flowering jasmine, *Jasminum nudiflorum*, is a deciduous shrub that grows laxly to 12 feet (3.6 m). The yellow flowers in winter are profuse and almost weatherproof.

the murkiest town, and I find it does better on a north-facing wall than on a south-facing one.

Usually grown as a climber – it will grow up to 12 feet (3.6 m) – it is far from self-supporting, its nature being to spray downhill, so that unless you can plant it at the top of a wall or bank and let it tumble down, you must attach it to your house wall with nails, wires, trellis or whatever supporting system you prefer. Leave the tops of the stems unpruned to droop gracefully. When the flowers are faded, pairs of very small trifoliate leaves will clothe the stems in a new dress, so that

discs the size of a florin which appear to gleam with an inner light.

Though it can be grown as an annual, honesty is more vigorous grown as a biennial, seed sown in early summer, thinned later, and transplanted to its flowering place in early autumn in the usual way, the plants 12 inches (30 cm) apart. Repeat the process the following year, after which you should have self-sown plants *ad infinitum*. The gleam of the pods is most pronounced in shady places, and as honesty likes light, dry soil, it is an ideal plant for growing under trees, where it shimmers and crackles mysteriously. It is lovely with green foliage plants, especially hellebores.

There is a white-flowered form, 'Alba', and a variegated form, 'Variegata', with green leaves edged with cream. Honesty

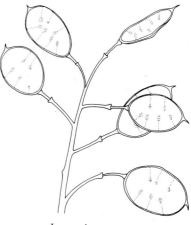

Lunaria annua

is a famous plant for drying, but the stalks must be picked in good time before autumn weather can damage the pods.

Honesty, *Lunaria annua*, a biennial or annual, has purple flowers in late spring. For flower arrangers the main appeal is the silvery seed pods on stems up to 30 inches (75 cm) high.

the plant has no dull moment throughout the year. At this stage it is advisable to shorten the stems which have flowered with secateurs, but not to cut them over closely with shears, as is sometimes done, for the plant will lose its trailing character.

Winter jasmine cuts well for the house, and needs a few stems of some evergreen plant to show off the yellow stars. I like it with sprigs of skimmia, or a small-leaved ivy.

Lunaria annua

Lunaria, moonwort, or honesty, is a plant better remembered for its seed pods than for its flowers, though these are quite decorative, growing in purple clusters in late spring; so are the toothed and heart-shaped leaves. But the seed pods are something special, transparent silvery

Mahonia aquifolium, the Oregon grape, is a thicket-forming evergreen that grows to about 3 feet (90 cm). This shrub flowers in spring and the berries reach their full size in autumn.

Mahonia aquifolium

This sturdy evergreen shrub is a native of woods in western North America where, because of the blue bloom on its fruits, it

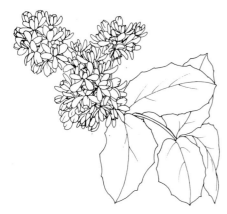

Mahonia aquifolium

is known as Oregon grape. It will form a dense thicket by suckering in almost any home you provide for it, including the shade of deciduous trees. I have seen it making a rough hedge on the ramparts of the Loire château of Amboise, and I grow my own single bush under a walnut-tree, which gives a fair picture of its versatility. It grows slowly, not usually to more than 4 feet (1.2 m), so if you plant it in the shade of your house it will not block the windows or invade the home.

The shrub consists of strong, upright stems decorated with glossy, pinnate leaves of a dark green which turns purplish in winter. At the top of each stem is a small leaf whorl with a tight cluster of flower buds inside. These form in winter to shoot up in spring into a spike of cheerful, yellow flowers. In autumn there are black berries covered with bloom. *Mahonia aquifolium* is hardy and will grow in any reasonable soil, but give it some humus at planting time.

Round my slowly increasing thicket I have naturalized as many spring bulbs as will accept the conditions, and luckily many do so against the odds. Snowdrops and the British native daffodil, *Narcissus pseudo-narcissus*, flower reasonably well, and *Helleborus foetidus* has seeded itself with its usual willingness to oblige.

Mahonia japonica

Mahonias are an acquired taste. I cannot now believe that I once thought *Mahonia japonica* too severe a plant for a romantic garden, for I now admire it above all other winter-flowering shrubs. It has both sculptural form and graceful flowers as well as the practical virtue of adapting to difficult conditions.

This mahonia is a large evergreen shrub, growing slowly to a height and width of 8 feet (2.4 m) or more. The main stems divide into many branches, each ending in a huge rosette of shiny pinnate leaves which are spine-toothed and must be carefully handled. In mid-winter drooping sprays of lemon-yellow flowers grow from the middle of each rosette, strongly scented with the boudoir smell of lilies-of-the-valley. The shrub is very hardy and never fails to flower.

It will grow in any well-drained soil and prefers shade to sun, which may scorch the leaves. Should these be damaged by

The sprays of lemon-yellow flowers of *Mahonia japonica* scent the garden in winter. The sculptural quality of this evergreen shrub, which grows to about 8 feet (2.4 m), gives it interest all the year round. It's very hardy but sun may scorch the leaves.

frost, leaf-spot, or other accident, a whole branch can be cut off above a young shoot on the main stem in spring – the shoot will grow at once and form its own rosette.

Flowers can be cut for the house, but if they are to last, whole stems with their leaves should be cut, not just little sprays

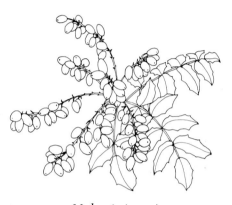

Mahonia japonica

of blossom, which will wilt. A shrub of this architectural nature should be grown as a specimen, either in the shade of buildings or under trees, provided these are not too dense and smothering.

There are some good mahonia hybrids, of which the best-known is 'Charity', but none has the rich scent of this species.

Skimmia japonica

This neat little shrub is a gift for the small garden, leaves, flowers and berries having

Skimmia japonica makes a neat evergreen shrub up to about 4 feet (1.2 m) high. There are scented flowers in late spring and female plants carry good crops of scarlet fruits.

Skimmia japonica

the trimness of a doll's-house plant. It makes a compact, evergreen mound about 4 feet (1.2 m) high with glossy, aromatic leaves, upright clusters of starry white scented flowers in spring, and shiny scarlet fruits which remain on the plant through the winter, for the birds disdain them. To achieve berries you must, however, have two plants, one of each sex, for the male and female flowers are not borne on the same bush.

The most attractive male clone in my view is called 'Rubella', with clusters of flowers which are red in the bud in winter, opening to white in spring. Its female companion could be 'Foremanii', and this will bear the fruits. Skimmias are rarely included in lists of winter-flowering

plants, but I find the sprigs delightful to pick for small vases, mixed with winter jasmine.

Skimmias grow best in shade and do well in town gardens, as they are slightly tender without protection. They will tolerate lime, but in heavily alkaline soil are improved by an occasional mulch of peat. If grown among trees, I suggest a ground-cover of *Galium odoratum*, or sweet woodruff, a charming little white bedstraw which is aromatic and was used by English cottagers for many centuries to strew the floors and keep down lice and fleas. An English native, it will grow even in the deep shade of beech-trees. Some alpine nurseries supply it, or a country friend might spare a few plants.

THE MOIST
SHADY GARDEN

Blessed is the gardener who has a piece of naturally moist land canopied with light shade, for he can grow some particularly lovely plants. But where, one wonders, are such favoured conditions to be found? They are most often seen in large woodland gardens, perhaps with water-falls and lakes, where the leaf-fall over centuries has created a soft mattress of acid soil; and a garden on a stream may have moist verges under trees.

But many small and unsung shady gardens have natural moisture, perhaps not used to its best advantage. A garden with underlying clay will be moisture-retentive, so long as the gardener, grumbling, no doubt, about the strain on his back, cultivates and aerates the top-soil. A garden on a slope will be moister at the bottom than at the top. A garden on normal soil can be made more moisture-retentive with the addition of peat. Moist soil is worth searching for and working well, for it is fertile soil and can be the home of many luxuriant plants, often with beautiful foliage.

So the damp, shady garden may be a gift of nature, or it may be partly created by man. Cultivation and mulching will be his most important contributions. The cultivation of clay soil will mean that rain gets to the roots of the plants instead of panning on the top; on drier soils, peat can be worked in at planting time, and be supported by subsequent mulches of peat, leafmould or compost.

LEFT A shaded pond-side planting can include many moisture-lovers, from graceful ferns to large-leaved perennials such as rodgersias.

ABOVE A splash of colour can give a welcome lift to the shady garden. Here a cream and green hosta complements a vivid azalea.

Should one water moisture-loving plants in time of drought? Here, I can only pose a question rather than give a final answer. If you have a source of soft water, the answer is certainly yes, and Mrs Fish, in her garden of limy clay, had many water-tubs to catch the rain. If you rely on tap water, often cold and hard, you may do more harm than good, and I have much evidence of lime-hating plants like rhododendrons being damaged by watering. I return to those two words which I have perhaps used too often for your patience: cultivate and mulch.

Aconitum napellus

Aconitum napellus

Aconitum, monkshood or wolfsbane, is a handsome, if sinister, plant which brings much needed blue to the garden in late summer when yellow can be too dominant. *A. napellus* is a fine species from east Europe and Asia much like a delphinium in habit – a hardy perennial with erect, tapering flower spikes 4 feet (1.2 m) tall, and plenty of glossy, finely cut leaves. The flowers are inky blue with hooded upper petals which give an air of mystery. There are several interesting varieties, of which the dark violet 'Bressingham Spire' is outstanding, and there is an unusual pale pink form called 'Carneum', but in pink the plant tends to lose its essentially secretive character. The aconite is a dangerously poisonous plant, particularly the root, which should be handled with great care and much washing of hands.

Aconites must have moisture, but given this are easy to grow in any soil in sun or light shade: they will even grow in rough glass, an addition to one's collection of plants for a flowery meadow.

If, after a few years, the flower stems grow weaker, divide the plant in spring and replant with manure. Plant in groups of three, five or seven plants, 18 inches (45 cm) apart.

Aconitum napellus is a hardy herbaceous perennial that produces spikes up to 4 feet (1.2 m) high of hooded blue flowers in late summer. Like other species of monkshood or wolfsbane, it is poisonous.

Alchemilla mollis

If I could have only one plant in my garden, it would be *Alchemilla mollis*, or lady's mantle. In sun or shade, in town or country, by castle or cottage, in chalk or leafmould, softening the edges of paving, underplanting roses, reflected in a pond, alchemilla always looks in harmony with her surroundings. This plant is sometimes listed as *A. vulgaris*.

A hardy perennial, the plant is graceful in leaf and flowers over a long season. For at least two months from early summer onward, feathery clusters of tiny, yellow-green flowers rise from clumps of decorative palmate leaves, each with a hollow in the centre which catches and holds drops of rain or dew. If the plant is sheared over after flowering, new leaves will follow, and perhaps a few late

Alchemilla mollis

Anaphalis triplinervis

This herbaceous perennial from the Himalayas is something of a freak in that it is almost the only silver plant which enjoys shade. The hairy felting of silver plants protects them from the drying effects of the sun, and *Anaphalis triplinervis* has felted stalks and leaves which are woolly on the underside, yet sun or shade suits it equally well, so long as the soil is well-drained, without being arid. It

Anaphalis triplinervis

the vegetables, and groups of alchemilla, among bushes of the red-and-white striped gallica rose, 'Rosa Mundi', make a loose edging to a flagged path. Another attractive scheme is alchemilla with madonna lilies in front of the purple-leaved shrub, *Cotinus coggygria*.

Alchemilla is ideal for picking and arranging with roses, campanulas, irises, or any other summer flowers.

Lady's mantle, *Alchemilla mollis*, is one of the easiest and most desirable herbaceous perennials. It flowers over a long season in summer. The leaf clumps stand about 18 inches (45 cm) high.

flowers. Alchemilla looks well planted in groups of three, five, seven plants or more, 18 inches (45 cm) apart which will soon grow into tough, weed-suppressing clumps, which are best divided every few years. The flowers seed almost too freely, and unwanted seedlings should be picked out when small.

Of the many gardens where I have enjoyed alchemilla I think particularly of the French-style kitchen garden at the Dower House, Badminton, Avon, where flowers for cutting are grown along with

Anaphalis triplinervis is one of the few silver plants that thrives in shade. This herbaceous perennial grows to 12 inches (30 cm) and the pale, yellow-centred flowers are borne in late summer.

is easily pleased and quite hardy.

This *Anaphalis* is not a dramatic plant, but makes a charming edging to a shady border. The clumps of silver-white foliage are perpetual but, being so light in colour, need the intensity of dark evergreen leaves nearby. Planted in companionship with bergenias, the two will give you a *chiaroscuro* picture all through the winter. The flowers grow in small, tight bunches, white with yellow centres, and are papery in texture like *immortelles*. They bloom in late summer, and if cut for the house will last all through the winter. Again, put them with dark, evergreen leaves, like those of *Elaeagnus* × *ebbingei*.

Plant the roots 12 inches (30 cm) apart and wait patiently, for *Anaphalis* is a slow grower.

Astilbe × arendsii

Astilbes have the somewhat artificial look of conservatory plants, but in fact they are quite hardy, and worthy of a place beside a pool with plenty of green round about to soften their hard colours. They are hybrids of several oriental species, providing a colour range of many different pinks, reds and white, the flowers growing in handsome plumes in summer from mounds of feathery leaves. 'Fanal', with intense red plumes, is a favourite cultivar and 'Venus' is a good pink. The leaves are usually bronze when young, maturing to mid-green, but in some forms are always bronze, and, being much dissected, look well against plants of more solid foliage, such as rodgersias, hostas, and hart's-tongue ferns, or with spiky-leaved plants, like the water-loving irises. The skilled plantsman would compose a foliage picture with all these plants, and more. In winter, 'the stems and seedheads turn a warm cigar brown' – I quote Mrs Fish, who did not cut her astilbes down until spring.

Astilbes need rich garden soil, either acid or alkaline, but it must be always moist, and naturally moist soil is a healthier medium than dry soil drenched with tap water.

Plant astilbes at least 18 inches (45 cm) apart, and divide them every few years, replanting with plenty of compost. The divisions can be used to increase the stock, for astilbe hybrids do not come true from seed.

Astilbe × arendsii

Erythronium tuolumnense

The erythronium most often seen in English gardens is the small European dog's-tooth violet, *E. dens-canis*, a bulb with pink, violet or white flowers in spring and broad marbled leaves. The petals are reflexed, like those of martagon lilies, giving the flower a nervous, do-not-touch-me air. This is the easiest erythronium to grow, being lime-tolerant and successful in sun or shade, but some of the American species are taller and more conspicuous, with a wider colour range, including yellow. They are, however, more fastidious in their choice of home. They need moist, leafy, acid soil.

If you have such a place in your garden, you might like to experiment with some of the American species, perhaps starting with the Californian *E. tuolumnense*, a hardy and vigorous plant about 12 inches (30 cm) tall. The flowers are golden with a brown ring in the centre, several to each stalk, with the reflexed petals of all the genus, and the large leaves are bright green and shiny. 'Pagoda', a hybrid, has larger yellow flowers and bronzy leaves.

'Venus' is of a softer colour than many of the hybrid astilbes. Most grow to between 2 and 3 feet (60 to 90 cm) high and all are good foliage plants with ferny leaves that are bronze when young.

The erythroniums are graceful small bulbs for woodland conditions. 'Pagoda', of which the Californian species *E. tuolumnense* is a parent, is a vigorous hybrid that will grow to 18 inches (45 cm) but it needs moist acid soil. The dog's-tooth violet, *E. dens-canis*, is lime-tolerant.

It will run about joyously among trees and shrubs, sending out underground runners which shoot up to form stalks topped with rosettes of evergreen leaves. Above the leaves loose sprays of little saucer-shaped flowers bloom in spring, very fresh and alluring in the light yellow-green colour which is typical of euphorbias. The whole effect is of a miniature flowering forest about 18 inches (45 cm) tall.

The plant prefers leafy soil, with or without lime, and will grow in sun or shade; it will if necessary grow in dry soil, but not for choice, and will be less luxuriant than where the soil is richer. It is almost hardy, but continuous frost may knock it back, though there are usually enough pieces left to renew the planting. I remember only one winter in my own cold garden where the losses were serious, and then it was so cold that even established hardy shrubs were cut back severely.

Plant *E. a. robbiae* in casual drifts, the plants 2 feet (60 cm) apart, with late spring bulbs round about, perhaps *Narcissus poeticus,* a pure white narcissus with a yellow eye.

Euphorbia amygdaloides robbiae spreads by underground runners and in spring the stems, about 18 inches (45 cm) tall, carry heads of yellow-green bracts. The leaf rosettes grow half-way up the stalks.

Erythronium dens-canis

Plant the corms in groups 4 inches (10 cm) deep and 6 inches (15 cm) apart, and leave them undisturbed to form large clumps. In a moist, leafy place shaded by deciduous trees they mix well with small English wild flowers, such as wood anemones, which will not outshine their modest beauty. A white flowering cherry would provide a perfect spring canopy.

Euphorbia amygdaloides robbiae

Though it is a first-class plant for ground-cover, this euphorbia is also highly decorative, well worth growing in its own right.

Gentiana asclepiadea

The willow gentian is an undemanding beauty. Tall and graceful, with trumpet flowers of true, intense gentian blue, it is long-lived, hardy and, unlike many members of the genus, lime-tolerant. It is surprisingly easy to grow.

It is a herbaceous plant with stems up to 2 feet (60 cm) long carrying pairs of slender, willow-like leaves with the flowers emerging from the axils. As the stems grow, they arch over, so that the whole plant is weeping by flowering time in late summer. Visitors to Sissinghurst Castle at that season have seen it in all its glory on the Azalea Bank, where it grows in large, floppy clumps among the scented azaleas which flowered in spring.

Gentiana asclepiadea likes deep, rich soil, and must have a moist, shady position, looking better among shrubs

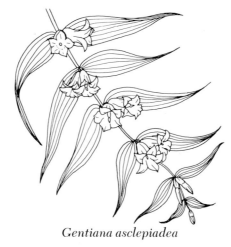

Gentiana asclepiadea

than in a border. Otherwise, it needs no special care. Plant the gentians 16 inches (40 cm) apart, or more if you do not mind the sight of bare earth for a few seasons, for the plant will in time form substantial clumps at least 12 inches (30 cm) wide.

There is a white-flowered form, 'Alba', worth growing if you have space for both colours, but the blue must have priority.

Hyacinthoides hispanica

The Spanish bluebell has undergone frequent re-christening by the botanists, and is better known as *Endymion hispanicus*. I presume that they previously called it *Endymion* after the beautiful son of Zeus who had the gift of eternal youth. There are many legends about Endymion, most of them disreputable, and Keats wrote an excessively long poem about him of which I will forbear to remind you of the first line, for you know it too well.

However that may be, *Hyacinthoides* is a tall scilla, a Mediterranean species which is much like the English bluebell, but larger in flower and leaf, and without the characteristic droop of our woodland flower, which is lovely in the wild but insignificant in the garden. It flowers in late spring and is a perfect bulb for naturalizing among small trees or shrubs. The bells are either blue, pink or white, and look charming in a mixture, perhaps under azaleas, though one of the nicest plantings I know is in a small town garden, where the blue flowers only are grown under the early-flowering yellow rose, 'Canary Bird'. I have also seen the bulbs naturalized in an apple orchard, and I sometimes think we grow apples as a shelter for

The willow gentian, *Gentiana asclepiadea*, is a clump-forming herbaceous perennial that grows to about 2 feet (60 cm). The blue and white flowers are carried on arching stems in late summer.

Hyacinthoides hispanica

bulbs or a prop for climbing roses rather than for the fruit.

The bulbs like a soil with a little moisture, and preferably some lime, but will grow in drier soil if there is shade. Plant them 3 inches (7.5 cm) deep in random groups.

The Spanish bluebell, *Hyacinthoides hispanica*, is easily naturalized in the light shade of deciduous trees and shrubs. The flower spikes, which are about 12 inches (30 cm) high, develop in late spring.

Meconopsis betonicifolia

To grow the blue poppy I would have to move house, but it is a plant of such dreamlike beauty that I sometimes think it would be worth it. A native of that legendary triangle of the high Himalayas where Tibet, China and Burma share their boundaries, it likes everything I have not got – lots of soft water, peaty soil, a cool, moist atmosphere and protection from wind. I include it in this book, devoted mostly to easy plants, because there are areas where it can be grown to perfection, especially in the north of Britain, and there are many gardens in Scotland, Wales and the northern counties of England which flaunt it for weeks in early summer. It is celebrated at the National Trust for Scotland garden at Inverewe. Although known to western botanists in 1886, the first successful introduction to Britain was made by Frank Kingdon Ward in 1924.

This plant has stems up to 4 feet

In the cool, moist conditions it enjoys, the blue poppy, *Meconopsis betonicifolia*, is one of the finest perennials. The sky-blue flowers are carried on stems up to 4 feet (1.2 m) high.

(1.2 m) tall; the flowers are tall and sky-blue with bright yellow stamens, several to a stem, and the leaves are poppy-like and bristly. Experts differ as to the best way to grow it, but I pin my faith on the Keeper of the Savill Garden, in Windsor Great Park, where this poppy is one of a thousand delights, who recommends that it be grown as a short-lived perennial. He raises it from seed, does not allow it to flower for one or even two years, until the plants are sizeable clumps, when they will last for three or four years. If you have the right conditions, put in the plants in groups 18 to 24 inches (45 to 60 cm) apart, cut off the flowers in the first year, and pray. It is a natural companion for candelabra primulas and other boggy plants.

Phlox paniculata

The garden in late summer is for the most part a place of hot colours and spicy smells, with a great many yellow composite flowers in their prime. But the lucky gardener who has a shady bed of rich, moist soil can grow *Phlox paniculata*, plants with the freshness of spring and a soft, sweet scent. The species, of North American origin, is purple, and many fine varieties have been developed from it in all shades of violet, red, pink and white, of which the pastel colours with a dark eye are particularly charming. All are hardy and perennial.

The flowers of phlox are much like primroses in form, and grow in large, crowded clusters at the top of leafy stalks with an average height of 30 inches

There are many colours in the varieties of *Phlox paniculata*, a valuable perennial for lightly shaded areas. The clustered flowerheads are carried on stems about 30 inches (45 cm) tall.

(75 cm). They need masses of water and a lightly shaded position will keep moisture in the soil and will prolong the flowering season. They are lime-tolerant, but chalky soils are too dry for them. They look perfect by a stream, and are massed with other water-loving plants in the Stream Garden at Hidcote Manor; if grown in a border they need mounds of good

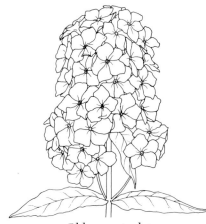

Phlox paniculata

foliage in front to hide their dowdy stalks. *Astrantia maxima,* with little umbels of rose-pink flowers over a long summer season, and elegant dissected leaves, would be an ideal companion.

Plant phlox in groups of at least five plants 2 feet (60 cm) apart in spring. (As they are very shallow-rooted, planting or dividing before winter is risky.) When they have grown a few inches, give them a generous mulch of manure or compost, and thin the shoots of large, old plants to get flowers of the best quality.

Polygonatum × *hybridum*

Solomon's seal is one of those life-enhancing plants which look tender and fragile, as though they required much nursing, but are in fact perfectly tough. They are hardy, perennial, will take to any soil, and spread readily if given a mulch of good leafy stuff in autumn, and a bit of shade. They like town or country life equally well. In fact, they behave just like lilies-of-the-valley and belong to the same family, the Liliaceae.

Nothing is lovelier in late spring than their tall, arching stems, some 2 feet (60 cm) tall or more, clasped by long pointed leaves all the way up between which hang clusters of small, tubular white flowers tipped with green. They are perfect for cutting, and even the most ham-fisted flower arranger, such as myself, will produce an elegant vase with Solomon's seal and some sprays of green foliage. Plant the roots 18 inches (45 cm) apart, perhaps with a group of hostas in front and a shade-giving shrub behind, such as *Spiraea* × *arguta*. Or, if the soil is moist enough, you could plant it with ferns. It is a mistake to plant with lilies-of-the-valley, as is sometimes

The arching stems of Solomon's seal, *Polygonatum* × *hybridum*, grow to about 2 feet (60 cm), carrying clusters of green-tipped flowers in early summer. This is a hardy perennial of poised charm.

suggested, for the two plants will spread at the same rate, and will have to compete for the available space.

Solomon's seal is a British native, and I used to pick it in an oak wood full of primroses, orchids and violets, which is now swallowed up by a housing estate, and I often wonder if a few brave plants have pushed through the rubble to surprise the fortunate householder.

Polygonatum × hybridum

Solomon's seal has a near and equally beautiful relative from North America, *Smilacina racemosa,* with similar leaves, but the stalks, about 4 feet (1.2 m) high, carry spikes of fluffy white flowers. *Smilacina* is more highly scented than Solomon's seal, but unfortunately it will not endure lime.

Primula florindae

This lovely yellow primula, known as the giant Himalayan cowslip, grows beside streams and in damp meadows in the mountains of Tibet. There it was discovered in 1924 by Frank Kingdon Ward and is now one of the best loved of the Asiatic primulas. A giant of the genus, it grows to some 3 feet (90 cm) high, with large umbels of drooping sulphur-yellow flowers with a creamy powder inside the petals, and the leaves are indeed like those of large cowslips.

In the garden, *P. florindae* must have moisture and a little shade, and prefers rich acid soil. Though not excessively demanding, in drier or poorer soil it will

Primula florindae, the giant Himalayan cowslip, grows to 3 feet (90 cm). The heads of drooping, lightly powdered flowers, appear in mid-summer, later than most of the primulas.

not make such a handsome plant. It flowers for several weeks from mid-summer and, like many plants which need moisture, solves the problem by growing very deep roots. One of the loveliest plantings I know is in a dell in a Kentish garden where *P. florindae* grows with *Rodgersia pinnata,* the tawny-flowered *Iris fulva,* other irises and primulas, and many ferns. In the background are amelanchiers for giving shade and autumn colour.

Put in the plants 12 inches (30 cm) apart with peat or decayed manure, and keep well watered until established. This primula seeds freely and hybridizes with other primula species growing nearby.

Primula florindae

Pulmonaria saccharata

Anyone who has passed a few spring weeks in one of the lusher parts of France has delighted in the common lungwort, *Pulmonaria officinalis*, which abounds by every road and stream. I choose *P. saccharata* for the garden only because the leaves are larger and more conspicuously mottled. Otherwise the plants are similar, herbaceous perennials with bristly, deep green leaves mottled with silver, and charming clusters of funnel-shaped pink flowers which turn to deep blue, the stems carrying both colours at the same time. They are of the borage family, hardy, and happiest in cool, moist places.

Many of the pulmonarias have spotted
or mottled leaves that make good
ground-cover. *Pulmonaria saccharata*,
a favourite of the cottage garden,
which grows to 12 inches (30 cm),
flowers in early spring, opening pink
but changing to blue.

The pulmonarias have all sorts of nicknames – lungwort (the leaves are said to resemble lungs, or to be a cure for lung disease), soldiers and sailors, and many more. *P. saccharata* has been grown in Britain for at least three centuries, a favourite plant of cottagers and

herbalists. It is an ideal ground-cover plant for cool borders, or beside a pool, the plants making a carpet which weeds cannot easily penetrate, and seeding freely. The pulmonarias look well with all moisture-loving plants, like *Doronicum*, *Caltha* (marsh marigold), or *Iris laevigata*.

Pulmonaria saccharata

There are varieties with all-white flowers, and others with pale blue flowers.

The plants should be placed 10 inches (25 cm) apart in groups of five, seven, or more, and I like to shear the leaves to the base when the flowers are over, or they may become brown and tatty. If cut down, a new crop will soon appear and will remain fresh for many months, so that the plant is almost evergreen.

Thalictrum speciosissimum

Thalictrum speciosissimum, a European relative of our native meadow rue, is a hardy perennial which brings grace to the summer border, where so many plants are stiff, if not positively coarse. A tall plant, up to 5 feet (1.5 m) high, it is all softness – soft, fluffy panicles of lemon-yellow flowers, soft blue-green leaves dissected like those of a maidenhair fern. Grown preferably in light shade, it brings an airy freshness to the garden at a sultry time of year.

Thalictrums are often happily associated with delphiniums; they seem as companionable as buttercups and daisies. At Kiftsgate Court, in Gloucestershire,

The fluffy lemon-yellow flowers of
Thalictrum speciosissimum are borne in
summer. This is a tall herbaceous
perennial, reaching 5 feet (1.5 m),
with blue-green leaves of fern-like
elegance.

they are grown with delphiniums and hostas; at Tintinhull, a small but celebrated National Trust garden in Somerset, with blue and mauve delphiniums and white herbaceous clematis. Another attractive species is *T. aquilegifolium*, a shorter plant with fluffy purple flowers and leaves like those of columbines.

Thalictrums will grow in any good

Thalictrum aquilegifolium

garden soil which does not dry out – the wild species are found in ditches and by streams. Plant them in groups 30 inches (75 cm) apart, working in plenty of compost or peat.

Trillium grandiflorum

The woodlands of eastern North America are the native home of these exquisite small perennial plants, also known as wood lilies or wake robin. Their three-petalled, pure white flowers appear in late spring above a trio of widely oval, veined, shining leaves high on the stalk.

Trilliums like deep, moist, peaty, acid soil and I have most often seen them naturalized in woods in Scotland, Wales,

Trillium grandiflorum 'Plenum'

The wake robin, *Trillium grandiflorum*, is a choice perennial for acid soils. All the plant's parts are in groups of three, conspicuously so in the case of the pure white flowers on stems up to 18 inches (45 cm) high.

Yorkshire, Devonshire and other parts of Britain with this kind of soil, notably in the National Trust garden of Knightshayes Court, in Devonshire, where a woodland is underplanted with small herbaceous treasures, as well as with peat-loving shrubs. These are ideal conditions, but trilliums do not demand them, and can be easily grown in any dampish place so long as there is no lime in the soil, which is poison to them. They have been grown

for many years in the town garden of an alpine specialist in Birmingham, who has them in the shade of rhododendrons. He told me that the key thing is not to cosset them but to leave them alone.

There is a pink form of this plant and a rare double form, of which the flowers have been likened to camellias, but it is not vigorous.

Plant trilliums 12 inches (30 cm) apart in good lime-free soil.

Veratrum nigrum

This stately and curious herbaceous plant has been cultivated in Britain for four hundred years, but is not widely grown today. True, it is a large plant, some 5 feet (1.5 m) tall and 2 feet (60 cm) wide, but it makes such a sensation in summer in a shady bed that it is worth finding space for a single plant, or a group of three, if

Veratrum nigrum

Veratrum nigrum is a tall herbaceous perennial of sombre beauty, with purplish-black flower spikes reaching a height of 5 feet (1.5 m). The large leaves have a splendid sculptural quality.

you can provide the right conditions. It is quite hardy.

The plant forms an impressive pyramid with spikes of tiny purple-black velvety flowers crowded up the stem as though a swarm of bees had settled there. The spikes shoot up from very large longitudinally pleated and deeply veined leaves. Like a piece of sculpture, these need space round them to be appreciated, so do not plant anything competitive near *Veratrum*. Self-effacing plants of medium size, like *Salvia superba* or blue rue will be the best sort of companions, or silver artemisias or santolina. There is also a white species, *V. album*, but neither the leaves nor the flowers compare with *V. nigrum* for sinister beauty. Incidentally, the specific name 'nigrum' refers to the root, which is black and poisonous.

Veratrum needs rich moist soil; likes some shade and will tolerate a little lime. It is recommended for woodlands as well as for a shady border, but few of us have this amenity, and mulches of peat or leafmould must do duty for those desirable woodland conditions.

THE POT
GARDEN

A large plant in a plain container of suitable proportions makes a bold accent in a
small or large garden. A foot or pedestal to the container can give a little extra
height and helps to make a neat finish. The mophead or hortensia hydrangeas are
particularly useful for late-summer display.

131

There are two ways of gardening in pots and other containers, and neither is right or wrong. Which you choose depends partly on the site of your little garden, but much more on your taste and experience of life.

One approach is to treat your garden as a breath of country air which has blown into town. This is a very English attitude, for the English are at heart a rustic nation, and their townsmen are transplanted countrymen. The English delight in villages, cottage gardens and wild flowers, and in making a pot garden, whether they have a whole terrace as their site, or a balcony, or nothing more than a window-box, they are likely to go for mixtures of plants and plenty of colour. They will use flowering shrubs, bulbs and bedding plants, and will have two plantings a year, one for spring and one for summer.

The alternative approach is for those with strong visual memories of the Mediterranean, especially of Italy and Spain. They will favour a formal arrangement and a smaller range of plant material, largely permanent and evergreen. Something as simple as two tubs of box or bay might be their choice, or a group of pots of architectural plants, such as *Fatsia japonica*, phormiums and ferns. If they want colour, there might be pots of choice shrubs, such as camellias or azaleas. Many city gardeners in the milder parts of the United States plant on these lines, and the Japanese courtyard is not

Choosing the background carefully can greatly enhance a brilliant mixture of flowers and foliage, such as this large pot of mixed petunias, daisies and *Helichrysum petiolatum*. Here the backcloth is a dark yew hedge.

ABOVE Clipped plants, such as box cones, arranged in pairs flanking an entrance or doorway, add an appropriately formal touch.

RIGHT The pot garden can include tender as well as hardy plants, those that would not survive outdoors in winter being treated as one-season extravagances or being given protection under glass.

dissimilar, with its accent on proportion and shape. Gardeners in the colder districts either confine themselves to bedding schemes, or take favourite tender plants, like camellias, into winter protection.

Both kinds of gardener are likely to have another ,element to work with as well as their allotted piece of ground, and that is a wall. Climbers, even tall ones, can be grown in containers and trained up trellis on a wall, making the garden seem more spacious than it is, and also lighter, for climbers with variegated leaves bring an illusion of sunshine. A town wall will also give frost and wind protection, and I have allowed myself some semi-tender climbers in my choice.

The techniques of pot culture are

Free-flowering plants that give a long display are especially useful in the small pot garden. This combination of petunias, geraniums and begonias in a restrained colour range will give a long season of pleasure.

much the same for all gardeners. Every plant must fill the pot, and be moved to a larger one as it grows, perhaps every other year. When mature, it need not be moved, but the soil must be renewed.

Every pot must have a hole in the base, and drainage should be provided from the start by putting a good layer of broken crocks in the bottom and filling up with well-manured loam, which will keep going for years if regularly topped up with fresh compost and liquid feeds. If loam is not available, commercial loam-based composts, such as those prepared according to the John Innes formulae, are good substitutes. I myself prefer these to light, peat-based composts, which are difficult to re-moisten if they dry out. Plants in the open ground can, to some extent, fend for themselves, but plants in pots must be watered regularly.

What material will you choose for your containers? I always prefer a natural material to a synthetic, and cannot endure the sight of plants in concrete —

there is more than enough of that in the streets outside. Simple clay pots with a minimum of decoration are ideal for most plants, but wooden tubs have a nice note of formality for clipped box or yew. A wooden window-box has more style than even the most convincing plastic material, and I suggest (following Miss Jekyll) painting it black to show off the flowers. The placing of containers on the ground is an art in itself, grouped pots on a terrace or in a paved courtyard having the quality of a still-life.

When planting a window-box I feel that simple arrangements, with no more than two, or at most three, plants are the most effective. It is difficult to beat small daffodils and grape hyacinths for spring, or purple and white petunias for summer.

A final word for those making a garden on a roof or balcony — remember that pots full of soil are very heavy, and be sure that you do not overload the structure.

RIGHT In the pot garden as in the open ground, simple effects are often the most telling. A single pot of marguerites conveys the fullness of summer.

BELOW The artistic grouping and arrangement of containers adds another dimension to the pleasure of the pot garden.

Abutilon megapotamicum

Among the most graceful of climbers, abutilons are not fully hardy in cold districts, but usually prosper in the shelter of a town garden. One of the smaller species, suitable for a terrace or balcony, is the Brazilian A. *megapotamicum*, with extraordinary nodding flowers like a Russian ballerina's costume – the red calyx is her bodice, the yellow bell-shaped corolla her skirt. They appear throughout the summer. Growing to at most 5 feet (1.5 m), this is a lovely plant for a pot in a warm position, and could be moved into shelter for the winter.

The more commonly grown A. *vitifolium*, from Chile, is hardier and taller, a soft-wooded shrub climbing to 12 feet (3.6 m), with mauve or white mallow flowers blooming over a long period and vine-shaped leaves. It needs the support of trellis on a wall, preferably in a position that gets full sun.

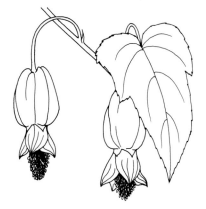

Abutilon megapotamicum·

Abutilon megapotamicum is a tender climber with graceful hanging flowers that grows to about 5 feet (1.5m) as a pot plant. The flowers are carried throughout the summer.

The Headbourne Hybrids are the hardiest of the *Agapanthus* but they need a sunny, sheltered position. The flower spikes are about 2 feet (60 cm) high, carried over the dark-green, strap-shaped leaves. The flowers, in shades of blue or white, make a welcome show in late summer.

(60 cm) high spring from each clump bearing large umbels of blue or white bell-shaped flowers which bloom over a long period. The leaves are typical bulb leaves, like those of large bluebells.

Agapanthus Headbourne Hybrid

Plant from one to three bulbs in a tub of well-drained soil and place it in full sun. If you find the pot looks too bare in spring, you could find space at the edges for some polyanthus.

Asplenium trichomanes

Among the aspleniums, a large group of evergreen ferns, two are widely grown in rock gardens and as pot plants. The maidenhair spleenwort, *A. trichomanes,* so called because of the resemblance of its pinnate fronds to those of the maidenhair fern, has a height and spread of up to 9 inches (23 cm). It is hardy but likes an alkaline soil, so include some

Asplenium scolopendrium

Agapanthus Headbourne Hybrids

There is a formality about *Agapanthus*, or African lilies, which makes them a good choice for a white-painted square tub. These hybrids are hardier than any of the species and are easy to grow, a joy in late summer, when stiff stalks up to 2 feet

mortar rubble in the compost.

The hart's-tongue fern, *A. scolopendrium,* or *Phyllitis scolopendrium,* another hardy species, is a familiar British native. It is the only true fern with undivided fronds – it has glossy, strap-shaped evergreen leaves with wavy edges. In the case of *A.s.* 'Undulatum' the fronds are even more deeply waved at the margin. The species is a vigorous plant which quickly forms a substantial clump in an urn or trough, and can be over-wintered and divided in spring, for it is quite hardy. It will grow up to 2 feet (60

The maidenhair spleenwort,
Asplenium trichomanes, is a lime-
loving hardy fern, which makes a
clump 9 inches (23 cm) high and
across. Ferns do well in shady
courtyard gardens.

cm) in the open, but probably less in the restricted space of a container. It likes quite deep shade and must have plenty of water, for it is in the rainy west country that it grows best, a common sight in the woods or stone walls.

Gardeners whose space is almost sun-less could make a fern collection from the many varieties available.

137

The glossy leaves of *Begonia semperflorens* can be almost hidden by flowers that are white, pink or red. This tender perennial is about 9 inches (27 cm) tall and is a good choice for window-boxes as well as for pots.

plants in autumn, unless you want to keep them in the house. Early spring bulbs can be planted immediately in their place.

Buxus sempervirens

A pair of box plants, meticulously clipped, makes a garden in itself, placed at the top of a flight of steps, or beside a house door. Box is never out of season, is evergreen, mercifully slow-growing, and perfectly hardy, smiling at frost or rain. It even has a faint scent when the small greenish-yellow flowers come out in late

Begonia semperflorens

This is a good plant for the gardener who designs in the country style, with a flowery mixture of bedding plants in summer. *Begonia semperflorens*, which grows not more than 9 inches (23 cm) tall, and has small flowers in slightly drooping clusters, is a natural choice for a window-box. The flowers are white, pink or red, and bloom from mid-summer until cut down by frosts. It is more graceful and blends better with other plants than the large-flowered *B.* × *tuberhybrida*.

The white forms contrast well with heliotrope, pelargoniums, fuchsias, and other plants of vivid colour. The red and pink forms can create some horrid clashes, so think out your colour scheme carefully if you use them; the lovely

foliage of ivy-leaved geraniums would make a good foil..Plant them in late spring in sun or light shade and discard the

Begonia semperflorens

138

spring. It can be planted as the centre-piece of a large pot of mixed plants, but looks much better on its own, and other pot plants can be strategically arranged nearby, such as tulips in spring and fuchsias for summer.

Box is a British native which has been grown in gardens for centuries for edgings and topiary; indeed, Pliny the

Clipped specimens of box (Buxus sempervirens) give a note of formality to the garden. The bright fresh green is constant.

Younger had a topiary garden at his Tuscan villa nearly two thousand years ago, with his name and that of his gardener cut out in box, and there is no reason why box in a pot need be a plain

Buxus sempervirens

ball or pyramid. You could try your hand at a peacock or dove.

In the open, box will grow into a tree, the wood being very hard and precious, but in a pot it can be kept to any size you want. There are variegated forms with green and gold or silver leaves, but in my view neither surpasses the plain green.

Camellia '*Adolphe Audusson*'

The range of camellias is infinite, with many species and hybrids to choose from, some with single flowers, others with semi-double or double flowers. *Camellia japonica* is the parent of many wonderful hybrids in a colour range of pink, red and white, nearly all suitable for pot growing. 'Adolphe Audusson' is de-servedly one of the most famous, with dark green, glossy leaves and very large, semi-double, blood-red flowers with gold stamens coming into blossom in early spring. It is an erect evergreen shrub of medium size, growing to at most 12 feet (3.6 m) in a container. Among other exquisite camellias for the contained garden are those belonging to the Wil-liamsii group. 'J.C. Williams', with blush-pink single flowers and yellow stamens,

Camellia 'Adolphe Audusson' has dark, glossy leaves to set off its blood-red flowers. A good height in pots is about 6 feet (1.8 m).

grows to about 6 feet (1.8 m). Being rather formal plants, camellias look well in the square wooden boxes called Ver-sailles tubs, which are topless cubes raised on four small feet.

Camellias will not tolerate a limy soil, so choose a peaty compost, but, unlike more acutely calcifuge plants, they can be watered with tap water. Do not plant deep, but just cover the roots with soil. If possible, site your tub by a west wall, which the sun will not reach until the morning frost has gone.

Camellia 'J.C. Williams'

Clematis macropetala

One of the delights of spring is to watch the fat, purplish buds of this clematis species opening into dusky blue, semi-double flowers nodding among a mass of fresh green foliage. It was introduced to the West from China in 1910 by William Purdom, who later travelled on an epic plant-hunting expedition through China and Tibet with Reginald Farrer, author of *On the Eaves of the World*.

Clematis macropetala is one of the most charming plants for a pot, either twining its way up a trellis or trailing over the rim to make a tangle of flowers and foliage on the ground. Its natural height is at most 10 feet (3 m). There is an attractive pink form called 'Markham's Pink', and if your pot is large enough, you could grow the two together.

Like all clematis, this species needs well-drained soil, preferably with lime,

'Maidenwell Hall' is a selected form of *Clematis macropetala*, a spring-flowering species that can grow to 12 feet (3.6 m). The semi-double flowers are followed by silky seedheads.

Clematis macropetala

and there is a case, when planting in a pot, for acquiring some limy soil in the country, and mixing it with decayed manure or compost and bonemeal, for clematis are hungry feeders. Otherwise, plant in a loam-based compost and give regular liquid feeds.

Pruning should be light, just a trimming of inconvenient shoots, and if you dead-head you will miss the silky seedheads which follow the flowers.

Clematis viticella

Clematis are so often grown as climbing plants that it is easy to forget how graceful they look trailing downhill from a pot, and no species is more appropriate for this than the deciduous *C. viticella*, bearing masses of small purplish nodding flowers and elegant leaves divided into leaflets. It has many varieties, of which my

Clematis viticella

favourite is 'Alba Luxurians', which I first saw in Mrs Margery Fish's garden cascading over a boundary wall to delight the passers-by. It has white flowers tipped with bright green. 'Etoile Violette' is a close rival, having violet flowers with creamy anthers, and there is the wine-red 'Madame Jules Correvon', with curious twisted, recurved sepals. All flower for about two months from mid-summer. They grow to some 8 feet (2.4 m), and might be trained over a low dome of wire netting in the pot to build up a firm structure, and then allowed to spray down. Grow them in well-fed, well-drained soil in light shade, and prune in early spring, cutting back the previous season's growth to a strong pair of buds.

Clematis viticella is a deciduous species, capable of growing to 12 feet (3.6 m), which produces large numbers of nodding flowers. It is as graceful trailing as it is climbing.

Coronilla glauca

This charming little shrub is not only evergreen, but ever-flowering. A native of southern Europe, it seeds itself with great freedom all over the woods near

Coronilla glauca

Cézanne's house in Provence.

Growing usually to about 6 feet (1.8 m), it is a mass of small, rounded, glaucous leaves with stalks carrying clusters of yellow pea flowers springing from the axils. The main flowering season is spring, but there are recurrent blooms at all seasons, including winter. It is hardy in normal winters, and, though safest in the warmer counties, there are mature and healthy specimens as far north as

The pea flowers of *Coronilla glauca*, an evergreen shrub growing to about 6 feet (1.8 m), are carried over a long season. There will even be blooms from time to time during the winter months.

The berries of *Cotoneaster horizontalis* make a fine autumn display on this sprawling shrub, which is about 3 feet (90 cm) high. The fish bone pattern of the stems is interesting even when they are bare.

Scotland. There is an equally attractive form with green and cream variegated leaves, but this is more tender.

Plant *Coronilla glauca* in light, well-drained compost, and give it a permanent stake, for it is a lightweight plant and liable to blow over.

Cotoneaster horizontalis

One of the most interesting of the cotoneasters, *C. horizontalis*, is an excellent plant for terrace or balcony, for its distinctive form deserves to be seen close at hand. A deciduous shrub, hardy and slow-growing, with a maximum height of 3 feet (90 cm), it has horizontal branches with shoots on either side giving the effect of a fishbone, and these can give a spread of up to 8 feet (2.4 m). It provides interest throughout the year, for in early spring come masses of small, pointed leaves, followed by clusters of tiny pink and white flowers; later, there are small

scarlet fruits, and finally the leaves turn scarlet in autumn. When they have fallen, you still have a distinctive shrub of eye-catching structure.

Seeds of this cotoneaster were first sent home from China by the indefatigable missionary Père David in 1870. Any good garden soil or well-drained compost will suit it.

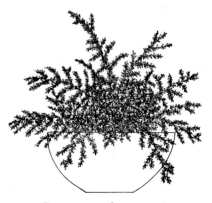

Cotoneaster horizontalis

'E. A. Bowles' is a fine selected form of *Crocus chrysanthus*, with bronze-feathered flowers standing about 3 inches (7.5 cm) high. Crocuses derived from this species flower in early spring.

excitement of *C. chrysanthus* is the multitude of varying seedlings to which it has given birth, usually slightly larger than the species, varying in colour from cream to deep orange, with delightful feathered markings at the base of the petals, on the outside. Both amateurs and nurserymen have selected and sorted these seedlings

Daphne odora 'Aureo-marginata' is a slow-growing evergreen shrub that is not likely to grow taller than 4 feet (1.2m) in a pot. The flowers are sweetly scented.

Crocus chrysanthus

E.A. Bowles, known as 'King of the crocuses', who published his magical *My Garden* trilogy in 1914, said that *Crocus chrysanthus* was his favourite of them all: 'One of the small-flowered species, it produces so lavishly that a few corms give a solid-colour effect in full bloom.' It is splendid in troughs, where its delicate beauty can be closely observed. Grow it in a gritty compost.

The species grows wild in Greece and Asia Minor, a somewhat globular golden flower usually flecked or feathered with dark purple on the outside. But the

Crocus chrysanthus

over the years, so that many are listed in the catalogues. 'E.A. Bowles' is butter yellow, feathered in bronze, 'E.P. Bowles' is deeper in colour, and the feathering is more clearly marked. They flower in early spring, well before the large Dutch crocuses which make such a fine show in our parks.

Daphne odora

I have found this daphne from China and Japan hardier than the Mediterranean daphnes, particularly in the form 'Aureo-

marginata', with green leaves edged with gold. A small, slow-growing evergreen shrub of sprawly shape, the branches divide into multiple twigs, each one topped with a rosette of smooth, shiny leaves with a tight cluster of mauve-pink flowers in the centre, like a child's bouquet.

The flowers are so heavily scented that in early spring you can smell even a little bush from many yards away. In the open

Daphne odora

ground the plant reaches a height of 4 to 5 feet (1.2 to 1.5 m), and rather more in width, but is likely to be smaller in a pot. A few small spring bulbs, such as snowdrops, grape hyacinths or scillas, could be planted at its feet.

Euonymus fortunei 'Silver Queen'

The leaves of this evergreen shrub of Japanese origin are so decorative that it has the value of a flowering rather than a foliage plant. They are of soft green with creamy margins, sometimes with a pink tinge, and the young shoots are plain cream, variegating as they grow. There are small, unimportant white flowers in early summer. It is a compact, slow-growing shrub, not more than 3 feet (90 cm) high, with the new shoots creeping sideways to hide the rim of the pot. There is a better-known form, stocked by many garden centres, called 'Emerald 'n Gold', with bright green and yellow

Euonymus fortunei 'Silver Queen' is a subtly variegated evergreen shrub that will grow to a height of 3 feet (90 cm). The flowers in summer are unimportant.

variegation, but the colouring is less subtle than 'Silver Queen', and clashes with anything pink.

'Silver Queen' would look well in a group of flower-filled pots, perhaps with pelargoniums or fuchsias, and white petunias. Plant it in well-drained soil, in sun or light shade.

Euonymus fortunei 'Silver Queen'

Fatsia japonica

This stately evergreen shrub is a plant for the town gardener who thinks in terms of form rather than prettiness and colour. When fully grown, it can be 15 feet (4.5 m) tall, and the theatrical quality of its strong, upright stems and huge, glossy, fingered leaves demands a conspicuous position, perhaps on a flight of steps or by a formal porch. The flowers are handsome panicles of round, cream-coloured umbels appearing in autumn, like flowers on the terminal shoots of ivy, which belongs to the same botanical family. *Fatsia japonica* needs some shade, and will grow in any good garden soil or a loam-based potting compost.

Since a full-grown *Fatsia* is extremely expensive to buy, you will probably want

Fatsia japonica

to start with a small plant, and to re-pot it every spring – its ultimate home should be a large pot of real quality. If grouped with other pots of evergreens, one of the

arundinarias, or bamboos, which are of airier, less solid texture, would make a good contrast, and a third member of the group could be a smaller evergreen, such as a variegated *Euonymus fortunei*. All these are plants from Japan, but I am afraid the Japanese tend to give courteous smiles at western attempts to reproduce their harmonious groupings.

Fuchsia
species and hybrids

Fuchsias, resplendent in their Russian ballet costumes, are the showiest of pot plants, giving a brilliant performance all summer long. Yet they are easy to grow.

Each nodding flower consists of a tube which opens out into four petal-like sepals which spread like a dancer's skirt. Below these are the corolla, usually in a contrasting colour – red over purple is a basic combination – and long, conspicuous stamens. There are many hundreds of fuchsia hybrids, both single and double, and the plants can be bushy, trailing, or standard, the first two being the most graceful in pots.

A number of fuchsias are hardy in

Fuchsia 'Tom Thumb'

a warm position, notably the species from which most hybrids are descended, *F. magellanica,* a tall, small-flowered plant in red and purple more suitable for the open garden than a balcony or terrace. But some fine hybrids have a chance of outdoor survival in a favourable micro-

The bold leaves of *Fatsia japonica* make it a strongly architectural evergreen shrub. It can grow 15 feet (4.5 m) tall. It will do well if it is placed in a lightly shaded position.

climate, such as 'Trase', with crimson tube and white corolla; 'Eva Boerg', a graceful plant with white over purple flowers on arching stems; and 'Princess Dollar', in cerise over a violet corolla, a bushy plant which is one of the most popular.

The fuchsia hybrids cover a wide range of growth habits and flower colour. Many combine well with other container-grown plants.

But overwintering fuchsias without benefit of a greenhouse is a chancy business, and most pot gardeners will throw caution to the winds and choose a gorgeous plant which they will grow for one summer only, planting it when the spring frosts are past, perhaps a cascading fuchsia for an urn or basket. (I do not usually care for hanging baskets, the sky being an unnatural setting for plants, but fuchsias do trail from them to good effect.) There is a lovely hybrid with white recurving sepals over a crimson underskirt called 'Cascade', and 'Citation' is a charming rose-pink over white.

Fuchsias should be grown in a loamy well-drained compost in sun or light shade. They need plenty of food and water, but do not swamp them, and pinch out the leading shoots to keep them bushy. The 'hardy' ones are well worth trying to keep through the winter. Protect the crowns with straw, and if they survive cut them down in spring.

Hedera helix 'Goldheart'

No plant produces more variety of leaf shape than ivy. From a handful of species, cultivars have been developed with oval, triangular, heart-shaped, arrow-shaped, crinkled or undulating leaves with many different veinings and variegations. All except the largest are suitable for the pot garden, especially varieties of the British native *Hedera helix*.

Ivies are hardy evergreen shrubby climbers by nature, clinging to their support by aerial roots, but they will also spread sideways on the ground, or trail gracefully from pots. In time, the young plant growing as a climber becomes 'adult', and bears flowers and fruits on the terminal shoots, but this is not really desirable, for the leaves lose their characteristic shape, and it is best to keep the

There is great variety of leaf shape and colour among the ivies. They give year-round pleasure when grown in containers.

plants clipped. If you want to cover a wall with ivy, put your pot near the wall and it will grow up it without support. In a more open place, the ivy will trail downward, and you can trim it as you wish.

In a town garden, choose an ivy not too sombre in colour. 'Goldheart' is cheerful and sunshiny, with small, dark green leaves with bright yellow centres and crimson stems. It variegates equally well in sun or shade, but if plain green

shoots appear, cut them out. It will grow to 5 feet (1.5 m) or more. An interesting ivy of shrubbier shape, for a pot only, is 'Conglomerata', dense and slow-growing, with leaves which are crinkled and wavy. For a row of ivy in front of a window-

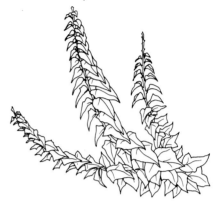

Hedera helix 'Conglomerata'

box, you must have a miniature ivy, such as 'Eva', with small green and cream leaves, or 'Shamrock', with small, dark green leaves like those of clover.

The less dense ivies will leave you room in your pot for some bulbs, perhaps daffodils for spring and lilies for summer. Give liquid feeds once a month in the growing season.

Hydrangea macrophylla (mophead group)

Mophead hydrangeas or hortensias are well-loved shrubs for a terrace, the flowers consisting entirely of large sterile florets without the disc of small fertile florets which distinguish the lacecaps, so that the flowers are dome-shaped, not flat. The leaves are toothed and deeply veined, a fresh, bright green when young.

Mopheads have for long been favourite pot plants, partly because of their striking flowers, partly because they are not fully hardy and if grown in pots they can be transferred to a greenhouse for the winter if the gardener has this amenity. Otherwise the pots can be sited in the shelter of a wall, where they should be safe in mild districts. In cold ones, they can be considered as a one-season

The mophead hydrangeas or hortensias, which grow from 4 to 6 feet (1.2 to 1.8 m) high, are handsome plants for late summer and autumn. They like shade and plenty of moisture.

Jasminum officinale

The 'casement jessamine' of Tennyson's *Maud* is a delicious plant to grow on a trellis near the house, for its heavy scent will waft about indoors as well as outside. A semi-evergreen twining climber from Persia, it is a plant of great elegance, grown in England since Tudor times, with

Jasminum officinale

small pinnate leaves and abundant clusters of little white flowers which are tinged with pink in the bud. It flowers continuously from mid-summer into autumn. This jasmine is hardy, but does best in a protected position in either sun or light shade, and is ideal for a balcony. It

pleasure, and replaced if need be.

Hydrangeas are among the last of the pot plants to flower, a delight for late summer. The colours are white, red, pink, blue or purple, but the blue varieties will turn red or pink in alkaline soil, and if you want blue flowers, plants in a standard loam-based compost may need dosing from time to time with a blueing powder. One of the hardiest varieties is 'Générale Vicomtesse de Vibraye', which is rose-pink or blue according to the soil, and the old cultivar 'Madame Emile Mouillère' is still hard to beat, a white hydrangea with a pink or blue eye.

Hydrangeas need rich soil, shade, and plenty of water – the roots must never be dry – but with a little care they are floriferous and healthy plants. The flowers can be cut off in autumn and dried for winter decoration, but in cold places it is better to leave them on the plant until spring to protect the young buds from frost.

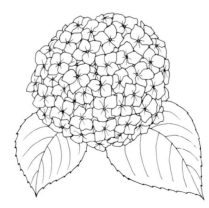

Hydrangea macrophylla, mophead

Jasminum officinale is a semi-evergreen climber with sweetly scented flowers. It can grow to 30 feet (9 m), but may be trimmed. It appreciates being given a protected position.

likes a well-drained soil and needs no pruning except a spring clipping of any shoots damaged by winter frost, or a trimming to size if it grows too large.

Laurus nobilis

The bay laurel of the ancients is a stately plant for a formal site. In Greece, it was sacred to Apollo and in Roman times stood guard at the gates of the Caesars, and is still often grown today in pairs by the front door of a house.

A dense, near-hardy evergreen with

Laurus nobilis

Container-grown specimens of the bay laurel (*Laurus nobilis*) are easily trained and kept to a height of 10 feet (3 m) or less. The leaves are aromatic.

dark green, glossy leaves, it will grow almost to tree size in a warm, sheltered garden, but in the confinement of a pot can be kept to any size the gardener wants, probably at most 10 feet (3 m), and looks best as a standard or clipped into the geometrical shape of a pyramid or cone. It carries small umbels of greenish-yellow flowers in spring. The leaves are aromatic and much used in cooking to give a tang to casserole dishes.

Bay laurel is hardy in all but the coldest gardens, and is particularly successful in towns. Plant it in full sun, out of the wind, using one of the commercially prepared loam-based composts.

Lilium auratum

Pots are not only for town gardeners. Increasingly, country gardeners are planting pots for architectural decoration near the house, or for growing plants which need special cultivation. For the gardener with limy soil, it is a blessing to be able to grow such lilies as are calcifuge in pots of lime-free peaty compost.

Lilium auratum, the golden-rayed lily of Japan, is a superb sight in a large, deep pot, the tall stems bearing masses of waxy flowers. The main colour is white but each petal has a golden stripe and crimson spots and the anthers are orange. It needs sun on the stems, but

Lilium auratum

The golden-rayed lily of Japan, *Lilium auratum*, which has stems up to 8 feet (2.4 m) high, makes a spectacular summer display. Pot-grown lilies of all kinds add distinction to a garden.

shade at the roots, best achieved with a mulch of peat, and lime-free soil, and should be watered with rain water. It will need a stake and liquid feeds through the summer. Plant from one to three bulbs 6 inches 15 cm) deep; they should flower abundantly for two, or possibly three, seasons.

Lobelia erinus

The lobelia is the quintessential plant for the flowery pot garden or window-box. A dwarf bedding plant usually grown as a half-hardy annual, it flowers all through the summer so long as the soil is kept moist. There are two kinds of *Lobelia erinus,* compact and trailing, both suitable for planting with petunias, fuchsias, and other bedding plants to make a bright summery group, though the trailing varieties are the more graceful, cascading over the rim of pot or box. There is quite a wide range of colours as well as the usual bright blue, including pale blue, crimson, violet and white. The compact 'Mrs Clibran' is brilliant blue with a white eye. All varieties have fresh-looking light green leaves. Lobelias can form an element in an all-colour mixture in a container, or in a simpler scheme, such as blue, green and white. Plant in early summer when the risk of frost is past.

Lonicera japonica 'Halliana'

This honeysuckle has grown in popularity in recent years, partly because it is among the most highly scented of all honeysuckles, partly because its flowering season is very long, from mid-summer almost into winter. I am more sceptical about its third attraction, that of being evergreen, for I find that the leaves become messy in all but the mildest

Lobelia erinus, either compact or trailing and rarely more than 8 inches (20 cm) high, adds a soft blue haze to the pot garden. It goes well with bedding plants such as petunias and fuchsias.

Lonicera japonica 'Halliana', a honeysuckle that grows to 30 feet (9 m), has highly scented flowers over a long season.

Lonicera japonica 'Halliana'

foot (30 cm) long, pinnate, very coarsely toothed, and of a rare colour, a true sea-green. The plant is shrubby and will grow to 6 feet (1.8 m) in perfect conditions, but would certainly be less in a pot. Sprays of brownish-red flowers appear in summer, but are of little interest.

Melianthus major is not fully hardy, but so distinguished a plant is a worthwhile risk in a reasonably sheltered spot. It should be protected in winter with a quilt of bracken or leaves, and if cut down by frost in spite of your care will probably shoot from the base in spring to provide glorious foliage for another season.

winters, and I would be just as pleased if they fell away. However, it is a wonderful, very leafy plant, with masses of rather small tubular flowers, open at the lip, of white changing to yellow. It is a vigorous twiner which will need trellis or wires, and requires thinning if it tries to grow out of control. Like most honeysuckles, it needs shading at the roots if grown in a sunny position, otherwise it will be happy in light shade. It likes moisture-retentive soil, and should be watered freely.

Melianthus major

Connoisseurs of foliage plants hold *Melianthus* high in their affections, for the leaves are ravishing – large and at least a

Myrtus communis

This beautiful shrub is not hardy in a cold garden, but may find a secure home against a warm south wall in the open ground or in a pot. Though it is said to originate in the Middle East, it is familiar to many of us as a plant of the *maquis*, or wild scrub, of the Mediterranean, along with cistus, lavender, sage and many other scented herbs.

It is a very leafy evergreen shrub, smothered in late summer with small, white, scented flowers which grow from the axils of the glossy, pointed leaves, which are aromatic. The flowers have five petals and are crowded with pale yellow

The jagged blue-green leaves of *Melianthus major*, a fine foliage plant, form a clump up to 6 feet (1.8 m) high. It needs a sheltered position and should be given protection in winter.

The common myrtle, *Myrtus communis*, an evergreen shrub with scented flowers, will reach a height of about 14 feet (1.2 m) when container grown. Fruits sometimes follow the flowers.

Narcissus 'Trevithian'

stamens, so that the whole effect is of a plant as starry as the Milky Way. In the open ground, myrtle will reach a height of 10 to 12 feet (3 to 3.6 m), but restricted in a pot will be perhaps 4 feet (1.2 m) tall, and can be protected with netting from winter frosts. The flowers are sometimes followed by inky fruits.

Myrtus communis

In legend, myrtle has long been associated with love, from the ancient Greeks, who held it sacred to the goddess of Love, to the present day, when a sprig is often included in a bride's bouquet.

Narcissus
dwarf species and hybrids

Dwarf narcissi are somewhat wasted in the open garden, for one cannot appreciate their miniature charm at ground level, and after flowering, the tiny bulbs are often forked over and lost, so that they never make large clumps. But in troughs and sinks, they can be intimately seen and every small feature enjoyed.

There are hundreds of varieties grown by nurserymen who grow for the rock garden, and all are just as suitable for pots. To select a few, there is the hoop petticoat daffodil, *N. bulbocodium,* a variable but always attractive species with little trumpets rounded like crinolines, the

varieties ranging from 3 to 5 inches (7.5 to 12.5 cm) high. There is the scented species from the Pyrenees, *N. requienii*, with several tiny flowers to a stem 5 inches (12.5 cm) high. And there is the slightly taller cyclamineus hybrid, 'Tête-à-Tête', with reflexed petals. All would look spring-like mixed with scillas in a wide container. Grow them in a gritty compost, planting quite close together, as you will probably be treating them as spring bedding plants, to be replaced after flowering with bedding plants for a summer display.

Narcissus bulbocodium obesus is a deep yellow form of the hoop petticoat daffodil, a variable species up to 6 inches (15 cm) high that is ideal for pots or sinks.

Nicotiana alata

If you love sweetly scented flowers you will certainly want the tall white tobacco plant in a pot or trough near the house, for when the flowers open in the evening

The tobacco plant *Nicotiana alata*, which grows to 3 feet (90 cm), is heavily scented in the evening.

their scent carries far and wide. They are tallish plants on stems up to 3 feet (90 cm) high, and may need a few twiggy branches placed discreetly among them to hold them up. Usually grown as half-hardy annuals, they flower in continuous succession from mid-summer until the frosts. They like rich soil and a sunny place, but will grow in light shade, in which case the flowers will be open by day as well as dusk.

There are a number of excellent

Nicotiana alata

varieties of tobacco plant, including the sophisticated 'Lime Green', much used in flower arrangements, and some dwarf mixtures in pink, red, yellow and white which remain open by day, but none of these has the rich, strong scent of the evening-flowering species, so you might have one pot of the latter, and a larger container for a dwarf mixture. All the tobacco plants are quite bushy, with large basal leaves, so there will not be space for much else in the pots, except possibly an edging of lobelias.

Osteospermum ecklonis

Nothing is prettier in the mid-summer months than a trough filled with South African daisies, for the flowers are exciting in colour and have a slight sheen on the petals. They are white above and bluish-mauve beneath and when open reveal electric-blue centres. They have a behaviour of their own, for they always look towards the equator, facing south in the northern hemisphere and north in the southern hemisphere, and they close at night and open in the morning. The leaves are narrow and toothed, and give off a musky smell when crushed.

The plant may be perennial in a very sheltered place, but is usually grown as a half-hardy annual. Plant 12 inches (30 cm) apart in a sunny place in light, well-drained soil, and deadhead regularly to prolong the flowering season. *Osteospermum ecklonis* is often grown in troughs in large gardens so that the charm and behaviour of the plant can be observed more closely than in the open ground.

The daisy-like flowers of *Osteospermum ecklonis* are borne in mid-summer on stems about 2 feet (60 cm) high. The unusual colouring of the flowers is more easily appreciated when the plants are container grown.

Pelargonium
regal and zonal hybrids

A pelargonium in a pot with its dense heads of flower, beautiful leaves, and rare intensity of colour, makes a visual impact which is unique.

Pelargoniums are tender sub-shrubs available in a bewildering range of hybrids, almost all from South African species. They are classified into several sections, of which only the zonal and regal hybrids concern us here; the ivy-leaved and scented-leaved species are described in the following entry.

The zonal pelargoniums are the ones most appropriate for bedding, though they are just as satisfactory in urns or window-boxes, where they get protection from the wind. Rather stiff plants, they have large heads of flat single or double flowers, the dominant colours being scarlet, salmon, orange, pink or white. The leaves are flat and nearly circular, patterned with colour; some have concentric circles of yellow, red and green, others are splashed or bordered with colour.

The regal pelargoniums are more spectacular, for the flowers are three-dimensional, not flat, often crinkled and blotched or feathered with a contrasting colour, and the leaves are longer than those of the zonals, usually cupped, and more deeply cut. The dominant colour of the regals is mauve, not scarlet. To name varieties when hundreds are available is invidious, so I will suggest just two in each section which are deservedly best-sellers – of the zonals, pale pink 'Morval' and 'Startel White', with serrated petals and zoned foliage; and of the regals 'Black Magic', a very dark mauve, and 'Princess of Wales', which is strawberry pink with white frilled edges and white centres.

Pelargoniums are easy plants to grow in containers, giving great effect for little effort. Plant them in a loam-based compost, give liquid feeds every fortnight when in flower, and water as needed, but not copiously. All pelargoniums need full sun or they will not flower well.

'Morval' is one of the many hybrid zonal pelargoniums, tender sub-shrubs with patterned leaves and flowerheads up to 3 feet (90 cm) high. They are as suitable for pots and window-boxes as they are for bedding.

Zonal pelargonium

Pelargonium
ivy-leaved and scented-leaved species and hybrids

The most graceful in habit of all pelargoniums, *P. peltatum*, with its cascades of glossy, ivy-like leaves, makes a garden in itself in a well-designed urn or pot. The trailing stems, which are rather brittle and must be carefully handled, can be as much as 3 feet (90 cm) long. There are many varieties, both single and double, mostly with flowers of discreet size about an inch (2.5 cm) across, in red, white or

'La France' is one of the trailing ivy-leaved pelargoniums, with stems up to 3 feet (90 cm) long. They help soften the edges of containers.

many shades of mauve or pink. 'La France', with semi-double mauve flowers, is especially delectable, flowering from early summer until the frosts. The stems do not branch naturally, so they should be stopped from time to time.

The scented-leaved varieties also have beautiful foliage, some of the varieties being bushy, others tending to trail. *Pelargonium tomentosum* is a species with hairy peppermint-scented leaves and tiny white flowers, *P. graveolens* has orange-scented leaves and pink flowers; both have the advantage that they make a mound of foliage before they spread out to trail over the rim of their container. Both can be brought into the house before the winter frosts arrive, cut back, and grown on as winter house plants. Grow all these leafy pelargoniums in well-drained compost in a sunny place.

Petunia × hybrida

The window-box gardener, pondering how best to use his exiguous space, would get glorious value from a row of

Petunia × hybrida

petunias grown as annuals. Their trumpet flowers come in all shades of pink and purple, in red, white, yellow or blue, single or double, frilled or plain, striped or bordered, with all the brilliance of circus costumes. The Grandiflora varieties have the largest flowers, the Multifloras are smaller, but more numerous and more given to trailing; all will flower for months on end, from midsummer until the frosts. The one drawback is that petunias do get washy in the rain, but the F1 hybrids are said to be more resistant, and their extra cost hardly matters when so few are needed.

Petunias need light, well-drained soil and should be planted about 9 inches (23 cm) apart, though very large plants will obviously need more space. I personally find the single varieties more shapely than the doubles, with their overcrowded petals, and two colours in a container are more effective than a rainbow mixture.

Most hybrid petunias grow about 12 inches (30 cm) high and flower freely throughout summer. 'White Joy' has full, frilly petals. Petunias are available in single and double varieties.

The evergreen sword-like leaves of *Phormium tenax* grow to a height of 4 feet (1.2 m) or more, making bold, fan-shaped clumps. It contrasts well with other pot-grown plants of lax growth.

Phormium tenax

This evergreen perennial from New Zealand has such an exotic appearance that it looks more appropriate near a building than in the open garden. Primarily a foliage plant, the leaves grow in fan-shaped clumps at least 4 feet (1.2 m) tall, are leathery and sword-like and of a deepish green, though there are varieties with purple leaves and others with variegated leaves boldly striped in green and yellow.

Phormiums need a sunny place and deep, moist soil, so the pot must be watered with special care. The species is hardy in most districts with the protection of a wall (the varieties are less reliable), and it is wise to pack straw round the crowns in winter. In some years the plants will produce tall flower spikes in late summer of dusky red flowers growing in panicles, but pot-grown plants flower only rarely, and it is the leaves which are the attraction.

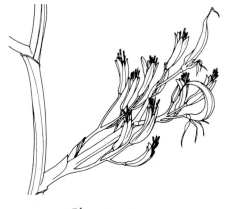

Phormium tenax

Rhododendron 'Cilpinense'

Of all evergreen flowering shrubs, the dwarf rhododendrons are among the most rewarding for the town garden or terrace. This doll's-house rhododendron makes a perfect rounded bush no more than 3 feet (90 cm) high. A hybrid of Himalayan and Chinese parentage, it is evergreen and flowers earlier than most rhododendrons, in mid-spring. The bell-shaped flowers are very profuse, growing in clusters of from three to five blooms, rosy red in bud, and white flushed with pink when open. The leaves are small and glossy. This rhododendron's qualities have won it all of the Royal Horticultural Society's top awards.

The plant is quite hardy, but on nights when frost threatens the flowers should be protected with netting or a cloth. Grow it in a peaty compost.

Rhododendron 'Cilpinense' is an early flowering hybrid that makes a neat bush about 3 feet (90 cm) high. Compact species and hybrids of rhododendrons do well as pot plants in town gardens.

Rosmarinus officinalis

The common rosemary is fully hardy in a sheltered place, a dense evergreen shrub from the Mediterranean with narrow, highly aromatic leaves which are glossy green above, white-felted below, and has light blue labiate flowers in late spring. Rosemary likes full sun and a well-drained, gritty compost. It is such an excellent culinary plant, especially with roast lamb, that the temptation must be resisted to pick it to death. It has for long held a place in the folklore of plants as a symbol of remembrance.

There are varieties with flowers in other shades of blue, and also in pink.

Rosmarinus officinalis

They are not so hardy, but 'Benenden Blue' is worth risking, a plant with very bright blue flowers introduced from Corsica by Captain Collingwood Ingram, or 'Cherry' Ingram, the celebrated collector of ornamental cherries.

The aromatic herb rosemary, *Rosmarinus officinalis*, makes an attractive evergreen shrub up to 6 feet (1.8 m) high. Most varieties have blue flowers. The leaves can be used in cooking.

Saxifraga Kabschia group

The cushion saxifrages are ideal dwarf plants for the trough garden, slowly forming tiny domes of green or silvery

Saxifraga burseriana is one of the Kabschia group, making a tight cushion an inch or so (2.5 cm) high. Like other cushion saxifrages, this looks well in a trough containing choice miniatures.

leaves with extremely pretty flowers on very short stalks in spring. One of the best is S. 'Jenkinsii', with masses of shell-pink flowers on red stalks; 'Valerie Finnis' is primrose yellow; S. burseriana is pure white and flowers earlier than the others; and there is an infinity of other species and hybrids to appeal to the gardener who is interested in alpines. These saxifrages look well in a trough landscaped with one or two rocks, and could be followed in summer by rock campanulas or *Phlox douglasii*.

They need a gritty, well-drained compost, preferably with lime, and do best in light shade, perhaps shielded from the sun by a rock; or the trough could be sited where a building would provide light shade. They also need protection from heavy winter rain, which is anathema to many alpines, and they can be covered in winter with a piece of glass propped up on stones to allow ventilation.

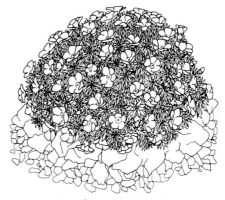

Saxifraga 'Jenkinsii'

Sempervivum tectorum

Sempervivums are plants for the collector, rather than the general gardener, but the specialist takes as much pride in his houseleeks as does the rosarian in his roses. They make an ideal pot or sink plant, being easy to grow and requiring little attention. They come from the mountains of central Europe.

Sempervivum tectorum, the common houseleek, is regarded as a symbol of good fortune on a roof-top. A succulent evergreen, it forms an attractive rosette 2 to 6 inches (5 to 15 cm) wide of fleshy green leaves tipped with dark red, and the rosettes join up to make mounded clusters. The flowers are not, to my mind, very life-enhancing, growing in starry pink bunches on fleshy stems in mid-summer; the plant dies after flowering. Houseleeks should be planted 6 to 8 inches (15 to 20 cm) apart and grown in full sun.

There are many other species and varieties of *Sempervivum*. A deservedly popular variety is *S.t. calcareum* 'Commander Hay', with large crimson rosettes tipped with green, and *S. arachnoideum*, the cobweb houseleek, has small, bright green rosettes laced with cobwebby white hairs.

Tulipa
species and dwarf hybrids

Small tulip species and their hybrids are some of the most charming of garden plants, but they tend to get lost to view unless they are in the confinement of pockets in a rock garden or of pots or troughs, where their miniature beauty can be appreciated. Nearly all are natives of central Asia. They range in size from the tiny *Tulipa tarda*, a mere 6 inches (15 cm) high, with white flowers with yellow centres, to *T. clusiana* (the lady tulip) with pointed white flowers flushed

with crimson on the outside, which can grow to 16in (40 cm). The *T. greigii* hybrids often have the added interest of mottled foliage, such as 'Red Riding Hood', a small scarlet tulip with leaves striped in green and purple, and

The crimson and green rosettes of *Sempervivum* 'Commander Hay', up to 12 inches (30 cm) across, make it a very bold plant. The sempervivums are succulents that need little attention.

Tulipa clusiana

The bright flowers of *Tulipa tarda* stand about 6 inches (15 cm) high and are borne in early spring.

T. kaufmanniana, a white, red and yellow tulip with reflexed petals, has many good hybrids, of which 'Stresa' is outstanding, with blood-red and yellow petals and mottled leaves.

Many of these dwarf species and hybrids flower earlier than the large garden tulips, and have a different visual value, being for close enjoyment rather than grand spectacle. I suggest that each species be planted by itself, not in a mixture, in well-drained soil in a sunny place, but if you like a tapestry, the tulips could be interlaced with grape hyacinths.

Yucca filamentosa

Miss Jekyll used this dramatic spiky plant to make focal points in her long herbaceous borders, but, surprisingly, a yucca can be just as successful in a pot. An evergreen shrub from the United States, it makes a striking clump of stiff, sword-like leaves about 4 feet (1.2 m) long, with spikes of flowers out-topping them in summer. These grow in panicles and are cream-coloured, waxy and bell-shaped, as spectacular in their season as any plant in the garden. The leaves are glaucous, but there is a fine variety with leaves striped in green and yellow. Yuccas like full sun and dry, well-drained soil. A big pot with a yucca could stand sentinel over smaller pots of dark-leaved evergreens, such as rosemary and hebe.

The flower spikes of *Yucca filamentosa*, more than 4 feet (1.2 m) high, top a plant of stiff and spiky leaves. Even as a foliage plant, a yucca makes a dramatic focus in the pot garden.

FURTHER READING

Books for the plant addict abound, but they need a little sifting. Some, though valuable, are too technical for any gardener but the specialist. Others, though delightful to look at, offer more to the eye than the mind. With diffidence, I suggest a short list of some of the best which will add to the knowledge and pleasure of the plant-loving gardener; but doubtless others will be published from time to time. I have placed them in alphabetical order.

W.J. Bean. *Trees and Shrubs Hardy in the British Isles* is the classic on its subject. In four volumes, it is very expensive, but is available for reference in nearly every good library.

Beth Chatto. *The Dry Garden* and *The Damp Garden*; the titles explain themselves.

Margery Fish. Read everything by this author, but begin with *Carefree Gardening*, or *We Made a Garden*.

Penelope Hobhouse. *Colour in Your Garden* brings to this difficult subject all the experience of a writer who manages a beautiful garden for the National Trust.

Gertrude Jekyll. *Wood and Garden* is the best Miss Jekyll book to start with, but all are excellent.

Robin Lane-Fox. *Better Gardening* is by a gardener-scholar who really tells you how to choose and use the best plants.

Christopher Lloyd. *The Well-Tempered Garden* is by one of the best of today's plantsmen, serious but wittily written. Move on to *Foliage Plants* by the same author.

Vita Sackville-West. *V. Sackville-West's Garden Book* is by the poet-gardener who created the magical garden at Sissinghurst Castle.

Graham Stuart Thomas. *Perennial Garden Plants* and *Plants for Ground-Cover* are two books by a master plantsman which are both encyclopaedic and delightful to read.

ACKNOWLEDGMENTS

The publisher thanks the following photographers and organizations for their kind permission to reproduce the photographs in this book:

1 Heather Angel; **2** Marijke Heuff; **6** Jerry Harpur/Octopus Books; **8–9** Jerry Harpur (Cobblers); **10** Philippe Perdereau; **10–11** Philippe Perdereau; **11** Linda Burgess; **12** above Marijke Heuff; **12** below left Philippe Perdereau; **12** below right Marijke Heuff (Mr & Mrs Dekker-Fokker); **13** Georges Lévêque; **14** Derek Gould; **14–15** Biofotos; **15** George Wright/Octopus Books; **16** Photos Horticultural; **17** left Derek Gould; **17** right A-Z Collection; **18** Derek Gould; **18–19** Harry Smith Collection; **19** George Wright/Octopus Books; **20** Photos Horticultural; **21** above Derek Gould; **21** below Photos Horticultural; **22** above Derek Gould; **22** below Photos Horticultural; **23** Tania Midgley; **24** Harry Smith Collection; **24–25** Photos Horticultural; **25** Harry Smith Collection; **26** above Photos Horticultural; **26** below Harry Smith Collection; **27** Harry Smith Collection **28–30** above Photos Horticultural; **31** left Derek Gould; **31** right Biofotos; **32** left Derek Gould; **32** right Photos Horticultural; **33** above Jerry Harpur/Octopus Books; **33** below Pat Brindley; **34** George Wright/Octopus Books; **34–35** Biofotos; **35** Photos Horticultural; **36** above Andrew Lawson; **36** below Photos Horticultural; **37** Tania Midgley; **38** left Harry Smith Collection; **38** right Tania Midgley; **39** left Derek Gould; **39** right Harry Smith Collection; **40** Derek Gould; **41** Photos Horticultural; **31** above Derek Gould; **42** below Photos Horticultural; **43** Pat Brindley; **44** left Michael Boys/Octopus Books; **44** right Photos Horticultural; **45** Harry Smith Collection; **46** above Bob Gibbons/Ardea London; **46** below Tania Midgley; **47** Tania Midgley; **48** left and centre Derek Gould; **48** below Jerry Harpur/Octopus Books; **49** Tania Midgley; **50** Jerry Harpur (Yeomans); **51** Marijke Heuff (Mr & Mrs van Bennekom-Scheffer); **52** left Photos Horticultural; **52–53** Biofotos; **53** Valerie Finnis; **54** Photos Horticultural; **55** left Tania Midgley; **55** right Michael Boys/Octopus Books; **56** left Photos Horticultural; **56** right Harry Smith Collection; **57** Harry Smith Collection; **58** Tania Midgley; **59** above Photos Horticultural; **59** below Jerry Harpur/Octopus Books; **60** Photos Horticultural; **60–61** Biofotos; **61–62** Tania Midgley; **62–63** Pamla Toler/Impact Photos; **63** Michael Boys/Octopus Books; **64** Photos Horticultural; **65** above Biofotos; **65** below Photos Horticultural; **66** Harry Smith Collection; **66–67** Tania Midgley; **67** Photos Horticultural; **68** Valerie Finnis; **69** Photos Horticultural; **70** Philippe Perdereau; **71** Marijke Heuff (Garden Mien Ruys Dedemsvaart); **72** Harry Smith Collection; **73** above Pat Brindley; **73** below Derek Gould; **74** Photos Horticultural; **75** right Harry Smith Collection; **76** left Pat Brindley; **76** right Jerry Harpur/Octopus Books; **77** left Tania Midgley; **77** right Jerry Harpur/Octopus Books; **78** Eric Crichton; **78–79** Tania Midgley; **80** left Pat Brindley; **80** right Photos Horticultural; **81** Photos Horticultural; **82** left Valerie Finnis; **82** below Tania Midgley; **83** Harry Smith Collection; **84–85** Philippe Perdereau; **86** above Michèle Lamontagne; **86** below Jerry Harpur/Octopus Books; **87** Philippe Perdereau; **88** Jerry Harpur (Pusey); **88–89** Philippe Perdereau; **89** Georges Lévêque; **90** Photos Horticultural; **90–91** Valerie Finnis; **91** Harry Smith Collection; **92** Michael Boys/Octopus Books; **92–93** Derek Gould; **94** Photos Horticultural; **95** above Photos Horticultural; **95** below Heather Angel; **96** left Michael Boys/Octopus Books; **96** right George Wright/Octopus Books; **97** Derek Gould; **98** Photos Horticultural; **99** left Tania Midgley; **99** centre and right Harry Smith Collection; **100** Heather Angel; **101** above Derek Gould; **101** below Photos Horticultural; **102–104** Photos Horticultural; **105** left Ardea London; **105** right Heather Angel; **106** Harry Smith Collection; **106–107** Derek Gould; **107–108** Photos Horticultural; **109** Philippe Perdereau; **110** Photos Horticultural; **111** Photos Horticultural; **112** above Derek Gould; **112** below Harry Smith Collection; **113** Photos Horticultural; **114** Heather Angel; **114–116** Harry Smith Collection; **117** Photos Horticultural; **118** Marijke Heuff; **119** Marijke Heuff (Mr Joop van den Brink); **120** Photos Horticultural; **120–121** Jerry Harpur/Octopus Books; **121** Tania Midgley; **122** Derek Gould; **123** left Pat Brindley; **123** right Tania Midgley; **124** Photos Horticultural; **125** left Tania Midgley; **125** right Photos Horticultural; **126** above Tania Midgley; **126** below Photos Horticultural; **127** Harry Smith Collection; **128** left Derek Gould; **128** right Harry Smith Collection; **129** left Photos Horticultural; **129** right Derek Gould; **130–131** Philippe Perdereau; **132** Michèle Lamontagne; **133** Jerry Harpur (Heslington Manor, York); **134** above Neil Holmes/Octopus Books; **134** below Andrew Lawson; **135** Karl Dietrich Buhler/Elizabeth Whiting & Associates; **136–137** Photos Horticultural; **138** Jerry Harpur/Octopus Books; **138–139** Harry Smith Collection; **139** Tania Midgley; **140** left Harry Smith Collection; **140** right Tania Midgley; **141** above Derek Gould; **141** below Photos Horticultural; **142** Harry Smith Collection; **142–143** Photos Horticultural; **144** Derek Gould; **145** left Tom Leighton/Elizabeth Whiting & Associates; **145** right Philippe Perdereau; **146** above Philippe Perdereau; **146** below Harry Smith Collection; **147** Harry Smith Collection; **148** Derek Gould; **148–149** Photos Horticultural; **149** Tania Midgley; **150** above Derek Gould; **150** below Pamla Toler/Impact Photos; **151** above Linda Burgess; **151** below Photos Horticultural; **152** Pamla Toler/Impact Photos; **153** above Pat Brindley; **153** below Harry Smith Collection; **154** left Tania Midgley; **154** right David Joyce; **155** left Harry Smith Collection; **155** right Photos Horticultural; **156** Pat Brindley; **156–157** Harry Smith Collection; **157** Derek Gould.

Lines from *The Land* by Vita Sackville-West, reproduced by permission of Curtis Brown Ltd, London, on behalf of the author's estate.

INDEX